The Complete Ninja Foodi

PossibleCooker Cookbook

2000 Days of Easy-To-Make Ninja PossibleCooker Recipes to Improve Your Cooking Skill, and Enjoy an Amazing Culinary Journey with Ninja Foodi Together

Eugenia Valero

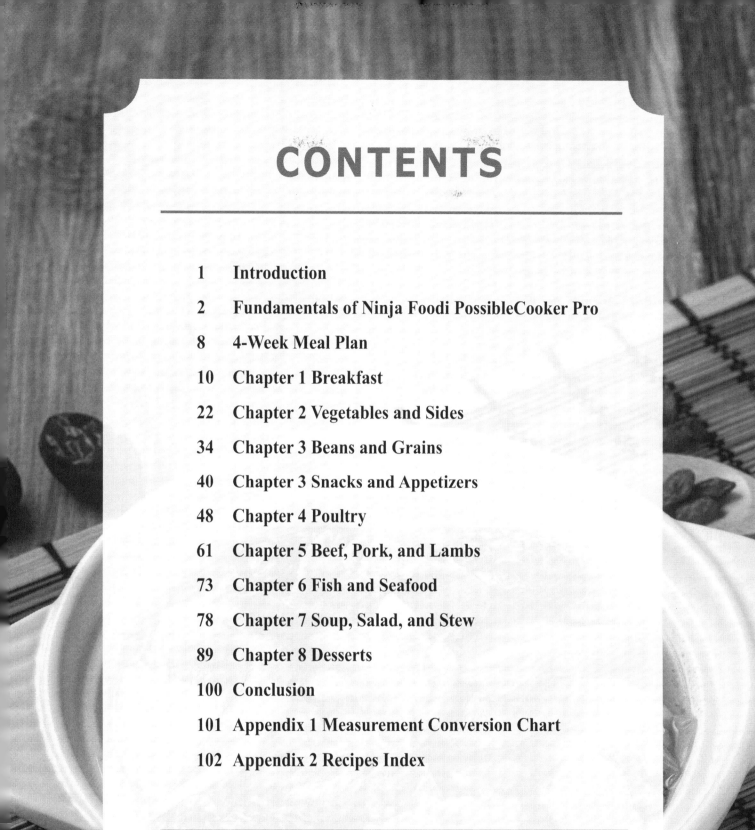

CONTENTS

1   Introduction

2   Fundamentals of Ninja Foodi PossibleCooker Pro

8   4-Week Meal Plan

10   Chapter 1 Breakfast

22   Chapter 2 Vegetables and Sides

34   Chapter 3 Beans and Grains

40   Chapter 3 Snacks and Appetizers

48   Chapter 4 Poultry

61   Chapter 5 Beef, Pork, and Lambs

73   Chapter 6 Fish and Seafood

78   Chapter 7 Soup, Salad, and Stew

89   Chapter 8 Desserts

100   Conclusion

101   Appendix 1 Measurement Conversion Chart

102   Appendix 2 Recipes Index

Introduction

Cooking is a great art with a secret language that we find interesting to share. This book will show a new innovation that can become your best kitchen companion, the Ninja Foodi PossibleCooker Pro. You need to master the secrets of this appliance to be sure you will get an amazing dance of flavors.

This appliance will allow you to cook endless amazing meals, from roasts to crispy casseroles. It is a game-changer that combines steaming, slow cooking, baking, searing, braising, and more, all bundled in one sleek device. It goes beyond being a mere device and promises to be your kitchen friend to transform your general experience.

Once you acquire the device, you are assured of several benefits. You get quality assurance, value for your money, performance is awesome, it has a nice appearance, you enjoy its versatility, and it is easy to use and clean. Thus, the Ninja Foodi PossibleCooker Pro brings efficiency.

This book will highlight several essentials, including:

- The basic fundamentals of Ninja Foodi PossibleCooker Pro.
- The advantages you will get as you use the appliance.
- Get an inside overview of its accessories.
- You will get a guide when acquiring it from the store.
- Maintenance is a good consideration when you need your gadget to stay longer. Thus, you get tips on cleaning and caring for the appliance.
- You will also get some frequently asked questions and other notes on the usage.

This cookbook is a wonderful guide. It goes beyond being a collection of recipes; it will unlock your kitchen's full potential, and you will enjoy one amazing and delicious dish at a time. Let's explore its possibilities.

Do you know a kitchen appliance that promises to transform your cooking experience? Ninja Foodi PossibleCooker Pro is here to assure you of the best experience, and you will understand the fundamentals before using the gadget. You might have seen the appliance in your friend's kitchen, heard more about it across the social media buzz, or seen it in the local appliance store you visited recently. Your curiosity might have heightened, and you need it in your kitchen.

From a mere glance, you may take this as another common kitchen device. But you won't believe it; the Ninja Foodi PossibleCooker Pro is a versatile kitchen appliance with a unique design that simplifies your kitchen adventure. Instead of wondering where you heard it from, take it in your kitchen and prepare those delicious recipes you always see online from your favorite chefs or cooking shows.

The sleek design and ability to steam, bake, slow cook, and other cooking tasks packaged in one appliance unifies this device. If you watched these capabilities on a cooking show or read a food blog, now is the time to bring it to your kitchen.

As we explore the fundamentals, take this gadget as your gate pass to the wonders of the culinary world. Unlock the full potential of this device by understanding the basics, whether you are a beginner or a seasoned chef. Enjoy the cooking and make it a wonderful experience.

What is Ninja Foodi PossibleCooker Pro?

There are many kitchen appliances in the market. As a brand, Ninja ensures that every kitchen gets the best in terms of simplicity, space utilization, and technology adoption. Both seasoned chefs and new cooks have a unique way to benefit from the Ninja Foodi PossibleCooker Pro. We ask ourselves, 'What is Ninja Foodi PossibleCooker Pro, and how does it redefine the cooking adventure?'

The Ninja Foodi PossibleCooker Pro is a multifunctional device that seamlessly integrates several cooking methods. You can think of it as a sleek and efficient kitchen appliance that combines steaming, baking, slow cooking, braising, and much more – all within one single device. The appliance brings the best cooking experience, where you can achieve an array of cooking tasks without much stress.

Everyone is talking about the versatility of this gadget. Both traditional kitchens and contemporary cooking spaces are ready to grab all the benefits of this appliance. The multifaceted capabilities make a nice go-to appliance. And what makes it win against other appliances is the ability to seamlessly transition between the various cooking functions. You can easily sear your favorite steaks to perfection, bake your sweet and savory casseroles, and steam delicate foods. It can easily adapt to different functions, making it a unique kitchen gadget to buy, especially with modern cooking where most people are busy. You will enjoy your home cooking and take it to newer heights.

Join this era of cooking with this appliance and convert your kitchen into a hub of creativity and flavor. Seamlessly converge efficiency, versatility, and kitchen innovation. Are you ready to unlock the door that introduces you to the world of many possibilities within the kitchen?

Benefits of Using It

The Ninja Foodi PossibleCooker Pro is here as a wonderful gadget revolutionizing how you do your cooking. It has taken into account the changing dynamics of technology, promising unique features to enhance your experience. You will get lots of benefits when you decide to use this appliance. Some of the benefits are:

1. You will enjoy redefined versatility:
The Ninja Foodi PossibleCooker Pro is an appliance that can serve

you in multiple ways and guarantees a seamless transition from one cooking function to another. You can bake, dehydrate, sous vide, keep warm, do your proofing, steaming, braising, slow cooking, and much more. All these functions are contained in one simple package. Such versatility gives you the ample calmness of enjoying a variety of recipes without needing multiple gadgets.

2. Time-Efficient Cooking:
Modern life has made many people busy, and time has become a very important factor to consider. Whenever you need to do your quick and efficient cooking, the Ninja Foodi PossibleCooker Pro comes to your rescue. You can prepare your food more efficiently as compared to the traditional methods. Busy families or individuals have a reason to smile.

3. Healthier Cooking:
Do you ever feel guilty about preparing or taking some of the meals, especially where you use lots of oil? You fear your body having issues related to excess usage of oil. With the Ninja Foodi PossibleCooker Pro, its capabilities have solved this, and you won't be guilty anymore. You cook your meals in a healthier alternative way, and there is no compromise on the flavor. Your taste buds get a delicious treat, and your body gets a healthy treat.

4. Consistent and Precise Results:
When using some other appliances or the traditional ways, you may have cycles where one day everything is perfect; then the next day turns out awkward. The Ninja Foodi PossibleCooker Pro guarantees consistency in your everyday cooking. You have precise temperature control and cooking modes, ensuring each dish is perfectly cooked. You could be browning meats, sautéing veggies, simmering sauces, or baking your delicious cake.

5. Reduction in Kitchen Clutter:
Your countertops won't be cluttered. No more overstuffing of your cabinets. Since the Ninja Foodi PossibleCooker Pro comes as a multifunctional device, there is no need for multiple appliances. This is a good way to streamline the space within your kitchen. And since it comprises the functions of many devices, you save in both space and the hassle of using different appliances.

6. Unleashed the Kitchen Creativity:
This is the best moment to go to your kitchen and experiment with different recipes. Make sure you try out the different functions, giving you an opportunity to see the different kitchen possibilities and come up with new recipes, cooking methods, and amazing flavors. You can try gourmet meals, sides, seafood, and the irresistible snacks.

7. Safe and Easy-to-Use Interface:
It is a user-friendly gadget free of cadmium, lead, and PFOA. The Ninja Foodi PossibleCooker Pro has an intuitive interface, and you can easily navigate the settings. The design of the controls is easy for anyone to use, from tech-savvy individuals to those who are starting their cooking adventure.

8. Energy Efficiency:
Energy conservation has become a necessity in the current world. The design of the Ninja Foodi PossibleCooker Pro focuses on efficiency. Given that it can perform multiple cooking functions, it minimizes the need for additional appliances, making your kitchen more energy-efficient.

9. Easy Cleanup:
The happiness of your cooking process is on top level whenever you have less cleaning to do. Ninja Foodi PossibleCooker Pro is good at that to give you peace of mind after enjoying your delicious meal. It has removable, dishwasher-safe components that make cleaning very easy. The pot is nonstick, allowing you to easily wipe out any messes.

10. Enhances Flavor and Texture:
You will realize that your meals' flavor and texture improve when you use the Ninja Foodi PossibleCooker Pro. Every dish is unique. Sit down and bring out a perfect sear on your steak. Your roast will have that succulent juiciness. You can also bake your sweet and savory casseroles.

Before the First Use

First, unbox the main unit by unwrapping and removing all the packaging material, stickers or labels, and tapes attached to the unit.
Unbox and remove all the accessories that come with the unit from the package, ensuring you carefully review the manual. Focusing

on the dos and don'ts is advisable to ensure everything goes smoothly. Check closely on the warnings, operational instructions, and essential safeguards to ensure no property damage or injury occurs.

Next, ensure the main base unit, the inner cooking pot, the spoon-ladle, and the lid get a good wash using a clean, damp, soapy towel. Warm water with a bit of soap does the trick. Do not try to immerse the main unit in water.

After washing, rinse them well and pat dry or air dry before the next cooking phase or before storing. If you're not up for hand washing, most parts are also okay to pop in the dishwasher.

Before you use the appliance, you need to turn it on and allow it to run for 10 minutes before adding any ingredient. Your kitchen needs to be well-ventilated. It is a good consideration to do away with any residual packaging substances and remaining odors. This step is safe and won't interfere with the performance of your gadget.

Step-By-Step of Using It

Slow Cook

1. Open the lid. Always ensure your hands are dry.
2. Plug in the Ninja Foodi PossibleCooker Pro.
3. Place the cooking pot inside the unit. Ensure the pot's indent lines up with the rear bump of the main unit.
4. Confirm all the accessories are in place.
5. Turn on the device using the power button.
6. Add in your ingredients and close the lid.
7. Turn the dial to choose the SLOW COOK function.
8. Utilize the +/- TEMP arrows to adjust your temperature by picking either HI or LO temperature settings.
9. Set your appropriate cooking time according to your recipe between 3 and 12 hours, adjusting in 15-minute intervals. (Note: you can easily adjust SLOW COOK LO time between 6 and 12 hours, and SLOW COOK HI may stand between 3 and 12 hours.)
10. Press START/STOP button to initiate the cooking process.
11. Once the cooking time elapses, you will hear a beep from the unit, and it will automatically transition to the KEEP WARM mode while counting up.

Sear/Sauté

1. Open the lid. Always ensure your hands are dry.
2. Plug in the Ninja Foodi PossibleCooker Pro.
3. Place the cooking pot inside the unit. Ensure the pot's indent lines up with the rear bump of the main unit.
4. Confirm all the accessories are in place.
5. Turn on the device using the power button.
6. Turn the dial to choose the SEAR/SAUTE function.
7. Utilize the +/- TEMP arrows to adjust your temperature by picking either HI or LO temperature settings.
8. Now, set your appropriate cooking duration according to your recipe. Using the arrow buttons, you can increase or decrease the time by intervals of one minute, going up to 15 minutes.
9. Ready to preheat? Press the start button. The screen will display 'PRE,' and a progress bar will show the progress. This process might take around 5 minutes but varies based on your chosen temperature.
10. Once preheated, you'll hear a beep; it is time to add your ingredients.
11. Lift the lid and arrange your food inside the cooking pot. Shut the lid, and your cooking starts with the timer ticking away.
12. You can press START/STOP button to stop the SEAR/SAUTE process.
13. Once the cooking time elapses, you will hear a beep from the unit, and the unit displays END.

Steam

1. Open the lid. Always ensure your hands are dry.
2. Plug in the Ninja Foodi PossibleCooker Pro.
3. Place the cooking pot inside the unit. Ensure the pot's indent lines up with the rear bump of the main unit.
4. Confirm all the accessories are in place.
5. Turn on the device using the power button.
6. Turn the dial to choose the STEAM function.
7. Now, set your appropriate cooking duration according to your recipe. You can increase or decrease the time by one minute intervals using the arrow buttons.

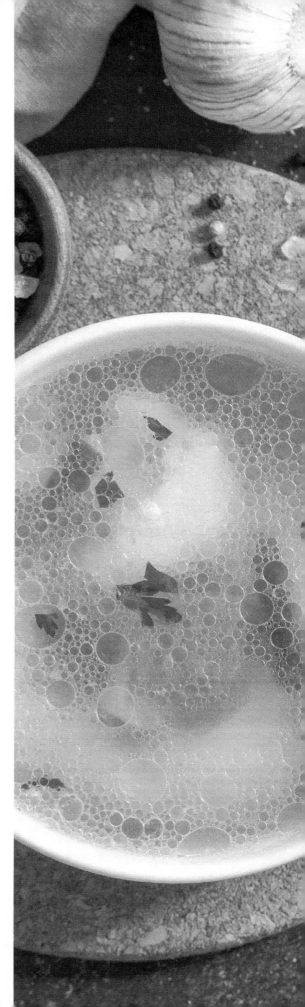

8. Ready to preheat? Press the START/STOP button to start. The screen will display 'PRE,' and a progress bar will show the progress. This process might take around 5 minutes but varies based on your chosen temperature.
9. Once preheated, you'll hear a beep; it is time to add your ingredients.
10. Lift the lid and arrange your food inside the cooking pot. Shut the lid, and your cooking starts with the timer ticking away.
11. Once the cooking time elapses, you will hear a beep from the unit, and the unit displays END. (Note: The unit automatically transitions to the KEEP WARM function when coming to the end of each cooking cycle.)

Keep Warm

1. Open the lid. Always ensure your hands are dry.
2. Plug in the Ninja Foodi PossibleCooker Pro.
3. Place the cooking pot inside the unit. Ensure the pot's indent lines up with the rear bump of the main unit.
4. Confirm all the accessories are in place.
5. Turn on the device using the power button.
6. Turn the dial to choose the KEEP WARM function.
7. The default temperatures will display. Utilize the +/- TEMP arrows to adjust your temperature by picking either HI or LO temperature settings.
8. Now, set your appropriate cooking duration according to your recipe. Using the arrow buttons, you can increase or decrease the time by intervals of one minute for up to 1 hour or intervals of 5 minutes for up to 6 hours.
9. Press START/STOP button, and the unit starts the count.
10. Once the time elapses, you will hear a beep from the unit, and the unit displays END.

Sous Vide

1. Open the lid. Always ensure your hands are dry.
2. Plug in the Ninja Foodi PossibleCooker Pro.
3. Place the cooking pot inside the unit. Ensure the pot's indent lines up with the rear bump of the main unit. Add 12 cups of water at room temperature.
4. Confirm all the accessories are in place.
5. Turn on the device using the power button.
6. Add 12 cups of room-temperature water to the pot.
7. Close the lid and turn the dial to choose the STEAM function.
8. Utilize the +/- TEMP arrows to adjust your temperature settings in intervals of 5 degrees to between 120 degrees F and 190 degrees F.
9. Now, set your appropriate cooking duration according to your recipe. The default is always 3 hours. Using the arrow buttons, you can increase or decrease the time by intervals of 15 minutes for up to 12 hours or intervals of 1 hour for 12 to 24 hours.
10. Ready to preheat? Press the START/STOP button to start. The screen will display 'PRE,' and a progress bar will show the progress. This process might take around 5 minutes, but it varies based on your chosen temperature.
11. Once preheated, you'll hear a beep, and the screen will prompt you with an "Add Food" display. It is time to add your ingredients.
12. Lift the lid and arrange your food inside the cooking pot. Shut the lid, and your cooking starts with the timer ticking away.
13. Once the cooking time elapses, you will hear a beep from the unit, and the unit displays END.

Braise

1. Open the lid. Always ensure your hands are dry.
2. Plug in the Ninja Foodi PossibleCooker Pro.
3. Place the cooking pot inside the unit. Ensure the pot's indent lines up with the rear bump of the main unit.
4. Confirm all the accessories are in place.
5. Turn on the device using the power button.
6. You need to sear the ingredients first using the instructions for the Sear/Sauté function.
7. Once the searing is complete, use stock or wine to deglaze. (Note: Add 1 cup of liquid to your pot for successful deglazing. Scrape the brown bits to the pot's bottom and mix with the cooking liquid.)
8. Pour the rest of the cooking liquid and your ingredients into your pot.
9. Turn the dial to choose the BRAISE function.
10. The default temperature will display. Utilize the +/- TEMP arrows to adjust your temperature settings if need be.
11. Now, set your appropriate cooking duration according to your recipe. Use the +/- TIME arrows to set cook time in 15-minute increments.
12. Press the START/STOP button to start the process.

13. Once the cooking time elapses, you will hear a beep from the unit, and the unit displays END for about 5 minutes.

Bake

1. Ensure the lid is open. Your hands should always be dry.
2. Plug in the Ninja Foodi Possible Cooker.
3. Set the cooking pot inside the unit, ensuring the pot's indent matches the main unit's bump.
4. Confirm all accessories are in place.
5. Turn the Ninja Foodi PossibleCooker Pro on using the power button.
6. Place ingredients into the pot.
7. Now, select the BAKE function. A default temperature will be displayed. Adjust it using the +/- TEMP arrows as needed. It should be between 250°F and 425°F. (NOTE: Adapting a traditional oven recipe? Lower your baking temperature by 25°F. And remember, frequent checks prevent overcooking.)
8. Decide on your baking duration next. With the +/- TIME arrows, you can set the time, increasing in 1-minute intervals for as long as 1 hour or 5-minute intervals for up to 6 hours.
9. Press START/STOP button to begin cooking.
10. When cook time reaches zero, unit will beep, and display END for 5 minutes. If food requires more time, use +/- TIME arrows to add time.

Proof

1. Open the lid. Always ensure your hands are dry.
2. Plug in the Ninja Foodi PossibleCooker Pro.
3. Place the cooking pot inside the unit. Ensure the pot's indent lines up with the rear bump of the main unit.
4. Confirm all the accessories are in place.
5. Turn on the device using the power button.
6. Place ingredients in the pot and place the lid on top.
7. Turn the dial to choose the PROOF function.
8. The default temperature will display. Utilize the +/- TEMP arrows to adjust your temperature settings in intervals of 5 degrees to between 90 degrees F and 105 degrees F.
9. Now, set your appropriate cooking duration. Using the +/- TIME arrows, you can increase or decrease the time by intervals of 5 minutes.
10. Press START/STOP button to begin cooking.

11. Once the cooking time elapses, you will hear a beep from the unit, and the unit flashes END on the display 3 times.

Tips for Using Accessories

Once you buy a brand new Ninja Foodi PossibleCooker Pro, you will find the following in the box:
- The 8.5-quart Cooking Pot
- Base Unit
- Detachable Spoon-Ladle
- Glass Cooking Lid
- Recipe Guide.

And when you cook using the Ninja Foodi PossibleCooker Pro, you will realize that there are a number of accessories that enhance your cooking and multiply your cooking experience. Let's check the tips on using these accessories.

Spoon-Ladle: It is a multifunctional tool that goes beyond serving. You can use it to taste, stir, and label delicious meals. Its unique design gives you ample time when using it in the pot.

Top Pot Handle/Spoon-Ladle Rest: Whenever you are not using the spoon-ladle, you can set it on the top pot handle for resting. This is good, especially in minimizing mess and organizing your space.

Cooking Lid: It is a preservative of your flavors. You add it on the top of the pot to seal in moisture during various cooking modes, ensuring flavor is infused in your dishes.

Side Pot Handles: These handles offer a secure grip when transferring the cooking pot.

8.5-Quart Cooking Pot: This is where all the magic happens. It is very spacious and allows for even distribution of heat. Preheat it before you add your ingredients. The nonstick surface allows for easy cleanup.

Main Unit: It acts as the brain of your cooking operation. Make sure you set it on a flat, stable surface, and there should be adequate ventilation to get optimal performance.

Control Panel: This is the command center. You can choose the cooking functions and adjust temperatures and time settings.

Helpful Hints

Here are the tips on selecting the appropriate ingredients.

1. Go for fresh produce. It could be succulent fruits or crisp vegetables (check for firm textures, fragrant aroma, and vibrant colors).
2. Choose the best fresh cuts of meats with a good balance of fat to enhance the flavor and tenderness. Go for bright, red coloration.
3. Select fresh, aromatic spices and store them well in a cool, dark place. Avoid the expired ones.
4. Go for fresh dairy delights (milk, cheese, or yogurt).
5. Do not stock expired grains or canned goods.
6. Select fresh seafood with firm flesh.
7. Always check with the seasons to ensure you take advantage of the seasonal produce. You can get fresh and affordable seasonal fruits and veggies.

Also, here are some practical tips.

1. **Safety First:** Always use oven mitts when handling hot parts.
2. **Ventilation:** Ensure your kitchen is well-ventilated to reduce smoke and odors.
3. **Experiment:** Get creative and test new recipes or your own composition.
4. **Storage:** Store in a cool, dry place. Do not add heavy items on top.
5. **Children:** Always keep out of reach of children when not in use.

Cleaning and Caring

If you want Ninja Foodi PossibleCooker Pro to last longer, you should pay attention to routine maintenance and cleaning. Here are some cleaning tips for this unit.

1. Cleaning of the unit should happen after every use. Before cleaning, ensure the unit is turned off, unplugged, and completely cooled down. Once your meal is out, leave the pot open for faster cooling.
2. A simple wipe with a damp cloth does the trick when it comes to the main unit or cooker base and the control panel. No fuss, no mess.
3. Hand wash the cooking pot. If any residues are stuck in the pot, fill it with water and give it time to soak.
4. For the other accessories, easily clean them by popping them in the dishwasher.
5. Air dry them before storage.
6. A golden rule to remember? Keep those harsh scrubbers and cleaning agents away. And, for goodness sake, don't submerge the main unit in water.

Frequently Asked Questions & Notes

1. Do I need to preheat it?
Yes, some functions require preheating. Preheating ensures even cooking.

2. Can I use metal utensils on it?
Best not to. Stick with wooden or silicone to prevent scratches.

3. Why won't my PossibleCooker turn on?
Check the plug and power source. Reset your circuit breaker if necessary.

4. The timer's not working. What do I do?
Reset the unit. If issues persist, reach out to customer service.

5. How often should I clean it?
Clean all removable parts after every use. Wipe the base unit when needed.

6. When do I add Ingredients?
After the preheat finishes.

7. There's a weird smell when I use it. Normal?
New appliances often have a scent. It should fade after a few uses.

8. Can I use the appliance for baking?
Yes. Make sure you use the right settings.

9. Why did the unit turn off?
If no function is selected within 10 minutes of turning it on, it shuts down automatically.

10. Why is the unit counting up instead of counting down?
The unit is in Keep Warm mode after completing the Slow Cook cycle.

4-Week Meal Plan

Week 1

Day 1:
Breakfast: Greek Frittata with Olives and Artichoke Hearts
Lunch: Slow-Cooked Drunken Beans
Snack: Delicious Onion Chutney
Dinner: Italian Chicken Thighs with Green Beans
Dessert: Vanilla Coconut Yogurt

Day 2:
Breakfast: Honeyed Apple Bread Pudding
Lunch: Spaghetti Squash
Snack: Honeyed Pineapple Chicken Wings
Dinner: Classic Steak Diane
Dessert: Chocolate Chip Lava Cake

Day 3:
Breakfast: Zucchini and Cherry Tomato Frittata
Lunch: Classic Harvard Beets and Onions
Snack: Perfect Mole Chicken Bites
Dinner: Tuna and Potato Casserole
Dessert: Apple & Peach Crumble

Day 4:
Breakfast: Tasty Hash Brown Casserole
Lunch: Quinoa with Brussels Sprouts and Walnuts
Snack: Meatball Biscuits with Cheese
Dinner: Wheat Berry Chicken Casserole
Dessert: Mixed Berry Crisp

Day 5:
Breakfast: Cherry and Pumpkin Seed Granola
Lunch: Flavorful Stuffed Sweet Potatoes
Snack: Classic Eggplant Parmigiana
Dinner: Delicious Beef Enchilada Casserole
Dessert: Peach Brown Betty with Cranberries

Day 6:
Breakfast: Morning Millet with Fresh Blueberries
Lunch: Tex-Mex Kale with Garlic Tomatoes
Snack: Fresh Chipotle Ranch Chicken Pizza
Dinner: Hearty Salmon Meatloaf
Dessert: Cinnamon Carrot Pudding

Day 7:
Breakfast: Spinach and Feta Quiche
Lunch: Herbed Garlic Smashed Potatoes
Snack: Sweet & Sour Smoked Sausage
Dinner: Savory Maple-Balsamic Lamb Shoulder
Dessert: Banana-Pineapple Foster

Week 2

Day 1:
Breakfast: Tasty Vanilla-Maple Farina
Lunch: Thai Green Curry with Tofu
Snack: Barbecued Pinto Beans
Dinner: Creamy Garlic Parmesan Chicken
Dessert: Cheesy Raspberry Cookies

Day 2:
Breakfast: Beet and Spinach Frittata
Lunch: Curried Squash with Garlic
Snack: Baked Sweet Potatoes
Dinner: Tasty Braised Beef and Pork with Green Salsa
Dessert: Lemon Butter Cake

Day 3:
Breakfast: Breakfast Strawberry and Banana Quinoa
Lunch: Buffalo Cauliflower Chili
Snack: Parmesan Spaghetti Squash
Dinner: Shrimp Scampi with Vegetables
Dessert: Comforting Maple Banana Sundaes

Day 4:
Breakfast: Delicious Eggs in Purgatory
Lunch: Cheesy Stuffed Tomatoes
Snack: Sweet and Sour Turkey Meatballs
Dinner: Barbecue Pulled Chicken
Dessert: Vanilla Lemon Custard

Day 5:
Breakfast: Basil Spinach Oatmeal
Lunch: Cabbage with Bacon and Pearl Onions
Snack: Asian-Style Meatballs
Dinner: Cheese Meatballs in Tomato Sauce
Dessert: Golden Almond Cake

Day 6:
Breakfast: Vanilla Zucchini-Carrot Bread
Lunch: Yellow Squash Casserole with Crackers
Snack: Fresh Fig and Ginger Spread
Dinner: Flavorful Salmon Ratatouille
Dessert: Mouthwatering Lemon Poppy Seed Cake

Day 7:
Breakfast: Sweet Breakfast Cobbler
Lunch: Garlic Cauliflower Mashed "Potatoes"
Snack: Spinach Artichoke Dip
Dinner: Pork Chops with Sweet Potatoes
Dessert: Yummy Pumpkin Spice Pudding

Week 3

Day 1:
Breakfast: Three-Grain Granola with Nuts
Lunch: Spaghetti Squash with Creamy Tomato Sauce
Snack: Homemade Stuffed Grape Leaves
Dinner: Cheesy Turkery-Stuffed Peppers
Dessert: Coconut Chai Custard

Day 2:
Breakfast: Apple Oatmeal
Lunch: Balsamic Brussels Sprouts with Cranberries
Snack: Classic Eggplant Caponata
Dinner: Italian Stuffed Meatloaf
Dessert: Minty Chocolate Truffles

Day 3:
Breakfast: Pumpkin Pie Breakfast Bars
Lunch: Buttered Cauliflower Mash
Snack: Cheesy Jalapeño Poppers
Dinner: Garlic Shrimp and Grits
Dessert: Simple Banana Cream Pie

Day 4:
Breakfast: Crunchy Keto Granola
Lunch: Tasty Southern Collards
Snack: Sweet 'n' Spicy Snack Mix
Dinner: Classic Jambalaya
Dessert: Tasty Peanut Butter Chocolate Cake

Day 5:
Breakfast: Classic Huevos Rancheros
Lunch: Brown Sugar Glazed Carrots
Snack: Lemony Chickpea Snackers
Dinner: Tender Shredded Beef Ragu
Dessert: Spiced Rum-Raisin Rice Pudding

Day 6:
Breakfast: Orange Almond Muffins
Lunch: Balsamic Braised Red Cabbage
Snack: Delicious Onion Chutney
Dinner: Monkfish and Sweet Potatoes
Dessert: Apple & Peach Crumble

Day 7:
Breakfast: Caramelized Peach Steel-Cut Oats
Lunch: Easy Braised Leeks
Snack: Honeyed Pineapple Chicken Wings
Dinner: Lamb in Coconut Curry Sauce
Dessert: Sweet Strawberry Pandowdy

Week 4

Day 1:
Breakfast: Buttered Cheese Grits
Lunch: Zucchini Ragout with Spinach
Snack: Slow-Cooked Cheese Dip
Dinner: Savory Mandarin Orange Chicken
Dessert: Delicious Chocolate Lava Cake

Day 2:
Breakfast: French Toast with Mixed Berries
Lunch: Vegan White Bean Cassoulet
Snack: Perfect Mole Chicken Bites
Dinner: Traditional Beef Cholent
Dessert: Rice Pudding with Raisins

Day 3:
Breakfast: Nutty Granola with Seeds and Dried Fruit
Lunch: Flavorful Mediterranean Vegetable Stew
Snack: Meatball Biscuits with Cheese
Dinner: Manhattan Clam Chowder
Dessert: Homemade Rocky Road Candy

Day 4:
Breakfast: Cream Cheese Peach Casserole
Lunch: Spicy Rice-Stuffed Peppers
Snack: Classic Eggplant Parmigiana
Dinner: Thai Panang Duck Curry
Dessert: Flavorful Double Chocolate Brownies

Day 5:
Breakfast: Coconut Almond and Cherry Granola
Lunch: Refried Pinto Beans
Snack: Chile Cheese Dip
Dinner: Hearty Red Wine Beef Stew
Dessert: Fluffy Blueberry Muffin Cake

Day 6:
Breakfast: Fresh Tomato and Feta Frittata
Lunch: Homemade Southwestern Veggie Bowl
Snack: Fresh Chipotle Ranch Chicken Pizza
Dinner: Thyme Salmon with Zucchini and Carrot
Dessert: Fresh Strawberry Cobbler

Day 7:
Breakfast: Simple Cheese Omelet
Lunch: Perfect Wild Mushroom Risotto
Snack: Sweet & Sour Smoked Sausage
Dinner: Palatable Turkey and Gravy
Dessert: Light Crustless Pumpkin Pie

Chapter 1 Breakfast

Greek Frittata with Olives and Artichoke Hearts   11

Zucchini and Cherry Tomato Frittata 11

Honeyed Apple Bread Pudding 11

Tasty Hash Brown Casserole 12

Beet and Spinach Frittata 12

Cherry and Pumpkin Seed Granola................. 12

Morning Millet with Fresh Blueberries 13

Tasty Vanilla-Maple Farina......................... 13

Pumpkin Pie Breakfast Bars 13

Breakfast Strawberry and Banana Quinoa 14

Basil Spinach Oatmeal 14

Delicious Eggs in Purgatory 14

Three-Grain Granola with Nuts 15

Sweet Breakfast Cobbler........................... 15

Spinach and Feta Quiche 15

Vanilla Zucchini-Carrot Bread 16

Crunchy Keto Granola 16

Apple Oatmeal 16

Caramelized Peach Steel-Cut Oats 17

Nutty Granola with Seeds and Dried Fruit 17

Classic Huevos Rancheros 17

French Toast with Mixed Berries 18

Coconut Almond and Cherry Granola 18

Orange Almond Muffins 18

Cream Cheese Peach Casserole 19

Easy Challah French Toast Casserole 19

Breakfast Quinoa with Walnuts and Apples 19

Fresh Tomato and Feta Frittata 20

Simple Cheese Omelet 20

Crustless Quiche Lorraine 20

Buttered Cheese Grits 21

Tex-Mex Scrambled Egg 21

Greek Frittata with Olives and Artichoke Hearts

Prep Time: 15 minutes | Cook Time: 6 hours | Serves: 6

1 tablespoon unsalted butter, Ghee, or extra-virgin olive oil
½ (14-ounce) can artichoke hearts, drained and diced
½ (12-ounce) jar roasted red bell peppers, drained and diced
½ cup pitted Kalamata olives, drained and halved
4 scallions (both white and green parts), sliced
12 large eggs

2 tablespoons heavy (whipping) cream
1 tablespoon minced fresh oregano or 1 teaspoon dried oregano
½ teaspoon kosher salt
¼ teaspoon freshly ground black pepper
8 ounces crumbled feta cheese

1. Generously coat the inside of the pot with the butter. 2. Layer the artichoke hearts in the bottom of the pot. Next, layer the roasted bell peppers, then the olives, and finally the scallions. 3. In a large bowl, beat the eggs, then whisk in the heavy cream, salt, oregano, and pepper. Place the egg mixture over the layered vegetables. 4. Sprinkle the feta cheese over the top and cover the pot with lid. Turn dial to SLOW COOK, set temperature to LO, and set time to 6 hours. Cook for 6 hours on low or 3 hours on high. Serve hot, warm, or at room temperature. 5. Slice any leftover frittata into individual serving–size pieces and refrigerate in a covered container for up to 3 days.

Zucchini and Cherry Tomato Frittata

Prep Time: 10 minutes | Cook Time: 6 hours | Serves: 6

2 medium zucchini, shredded
1 teaspoon kosher salt, divided
1 tablespoon extra-virgin olive oil
12 large eggs
3 tablespoons heavy (whipping) cream
3 tablespoons finely chopped fresh parsley

1 tablespoon fresh thyme or 1 teaspoon dried thyme
½ teaspoon paprika
½ teaspoon freshly ground black pepper
6 ounces ricotta cheese
12 cherry tomatoes, halved
½ cup grated Parmesan cheese

1. In a colander set in the sink, toss the shredded zucchini with ½ teaspoon of salt. Let the zucchini sit for a few minutes, then squeeze out the excess liquid with your hands. 2. Generously coat the inside of the pot with the olive oil. 3. In a large bowl, beat the eggs, then whisk in the heavy cream, parsley, paprika, pepper, thyme, and the remaining ½ teaspoon of salt. 4. Add the zucchini and stir to combine well. Transfer the mixture to the prepared pot. 5. Using a large spoon, dollop the ricotta cheese into the egg mixture, distributing it evenly. 6. Top with the tomatoes and sprinkle the Parmesan cheese over the top. Cover the pot with lid. Turn dial to SLOW COOK, set temperature to LO, and set time to 6 hours. Cook for 6 hours on low or 3 hours on high. Serve hot, warm, or at room temperature. 7. Slice any leftover frittata into individual serving–size pieces and refrigerate in a covered container for up to 3 days.

Honeyed Apple Bread Pudding

Prep Time: 10 minutes | Cook Time: 3½-4½ hours | Serves: 6

2 apples, chopped
¼ cup apple juice
⅓ cup brown sugar
¼ cup honey
2 tablespoons butter, melted
4 eggs, beaten

⅓ cup whole milk
1 teaspoon vanilla
½ teaspoon cinnamon
8 slices raisin swirl bread
½ cup raisins

1. In a medium saucepan, combine apples with apple juice. Bring to a simmer and simmer, stirring frequently, 5 minutes. Remove from heat and set aside for 10 minutes. Drain apples, reserving juice. 2. In a small bowl, combine the honey, brown sugar, and butter, mix well, and set aside. 3. In a large bowl, combine the reserved apple juice, milk, eggs, vanilla, and cinnamon, beat well, and set aside. 4. Cut bread slices into cubes. In the pot, layer the bread cubes, raisins, apples, and the brown sugar mixture. Repeat layers. Pour egg mixture over all and cover with lid. 5. Turn dial to SLOW COOK, set temperature to HI, and set time to 3½ hours. Cook for 3½ to 4½ hours until pudding is set. 6. When cooking is complete, let cool for 30 minutes and serve.

Tasty Hash Brown Casserole
Prep Time: 10 minutes | Cook Time: 10-12 hours | Serves: 6

1 tablespoon butter
1 onion, chopped
2 cloves garlic, minced
6 cups frozen hash brown potatoes
¾ cup shredded mozzarella cheese
6 eggs

½ teaspoon dried thyme leaves
½ teaspoon salt
⅛ teaspoon pepper
1 (5-ounce) can evaporated milk
½ cup shredded Cheddar cheese
2 tablespoons chopped parsley

1. Spray inside of the pot with nonstick cooking spray. 2. In a skillet over medium heat, melt the butter. Add onion and garlic, cook, and stir until crisp and tender. Let cool for about 10 minutes. 3. Place ⅓ of the frozen hash brown potatoes in the pot. Add ⅓ of onion mixture and ⅓ of the mozzarella cheese. Repeat layers, ending with the cheese. 4. In a medium bowl, beat eggs, seasonings, and milk until blended. Pour over the ingredients in the pot and cover with lid. 5. Turn dial to SLOW COOK, set temperature to LO, and set time to 10 hours. Cook for 10 to 12 hours until set. 6. Sprinkle with Cheddar cheese and parsley, let stand until cheese melts, and serve.

Beet and Spinach Frittata
Prep Time: 15 minutes | Cook Time: 5-7 hours | Serves: 4-6

1 tablespoon extra-virgin olive oil
8 large eggs
1 cup packed fresh spinach leaves, chopped
1 cup diced peeled golden beets
½ medium onion, diced

¼ cup unsweetened almond milk
¾ teaspoon sea salt
½ teaspoon garlic powder
½ teaspoon dried basil leaves
Freshly ground black pepper

1. Coat the pot with the olive oil. 2. In a large bowl, combine the eggs, beets, onion, spinach, almond milk, garlic powder, salt, and basil, and season with pepper. Whisk together and pour the custard into the pot. 3. Cover with the lid. Turn dial to SLOW COOK, set temperature to LO, and set time to 5 hours. Cook for 5 to 7 hours or until the eggs are completely set. 4. When cooking is complete, serve.

Cherry and Pumpkin Seed Granola
Prep Time: 15 minutes | Cook Time: 5-6 hours | Serves: 4-6

5 tablespoons melted coconut oil, divided
1 cup unsweetened shredded coconut
1 cup rolled oats
1 cup pecans
½ cup pumpkin seeds
1 ripe banana

1 tablespoon vanilla extract
½ teaspoon sea salt
½ teaspoon ground cinnamon
½ teaspoon ground ginger
1 cup dried sour cherries

1. Coat the pot with 1 tablespoon of coconut oil. 2. In your pot, toss together the oats, coconut, pecans, and pumpkin seeds. 3. In a small bowl, mash the banana with the remaining ¼ cup of melted coconut oil, the vanilla, cinnamon, salt, and ginger. 4. Add the liquid ingredients to the granola mixture and stir well to combine. 5. Cover with the lid. Turn dial to SLOW COOK, set temperature to LO, and set time to 5 hours. Cook for 5 to 6 hours. 6. When the cooking is finished, stir in the cherries. 7. Spread the granola on a flat surface or baking sheet to cool and dry completely before storing in airtight containers. Stored in a cool place, this will keep up to six months.

Morning Millet with Fresh Blueberries

Prep Time: 15 minutes | Cook Time: 7-8 hours | Serves: 4

1 cup millet
2 cups water
2 cups full-fat coconut milk
½ teaspoon sea salt

½ teaspoon ground cinnamon
½ teaspoon ground ginger
¼ teaspoon vanilla extract
½ cup fresh blueberries

1. In the pot, combine the millet, water, salt, cinnamon, coconut milk, ginger, and vanilla. Stir well and cover with lid. 2. Turn dial to SLOW COOK, set temperature to LO, and set time to 7 hours. Cook for 7 to 8 hours. 3. Stir in the blueberries to warm at the end and serve.

Tasty Vanilla-Maple Farina

Prep Time: 5 minutes | Cook Time: 8 hours | Serves: 4

¾ cup Cream of Wheat
½ teaspoon sea salt
2 cups water

2 cups 2 percent milk
¾ teaspoon vanilla extract
¼ cup pure maple syrup, plus more for topping

1. In the pot, combine the Cream of Wheat, salt, milk, vanilla, water, and maple syrup. Cover with the lid. 2. Turn dial to SLOW COOK, set temperature to LO, and set time to 8 hours. Cook until thick and creamy. 3. When cooking is complete, serve the farina warm, topped with maple syrup. 4. Refrigerate leftovers for up to 5 days, or freeze for up to 2 months.

Pumpkin Pie Breakfast Bars

Prep Time: 15 minutes | Cook Time: 3 hours | Serves: 8

For the Crust
5 tablespoons butter, softened, divided
¾ cup unsweetened shredded coconut
For the Filling
1 (28-ounce) can pumpkin purée
1 cup heavy (whipping) cream
4 eggs
1 ounce protein powder
1 teaspoon pure vanilla extract
4 drops liquid stevia

½ cup almond flour
¼ cup granulated erythritol

1 teaspoon ground cinnamon
½ teaspoon ground ginger
¼ teaspoon ground nutmeg
Pinch ground cloves
Pinch salt

For the crust: 1. Lightly grease the bottom of pot with 1 tablespoon of the butter. 2. In a small bowl, stir together the coconut, erythritol, almond flour, and remaining butter until the mixture forms into coarse crumbs. 3. Press the crumbs into the bottom of the pot evenly to form a crust.

For the filling: 1. In a medium bowl, stir together the eggs, protein powder, pumpkin, heavy cream, vanilla, stevia, cinnamon, nutmeg, cloves, ginger, and salt until well blended. 2. Spread the filling evenly over the crust and cover with lid. 3. Turn dial to SLOW COOK, set temperature to LO, and set time to 3 hours. 4. When cooking is complete, remove the lid to cool for 30 minutes. Then place the pot in the refrigerator until completely chilled, about 2 hours. 5. Cut into squares and store them in the refrigerator in a sealed container for up to 5 days.

Breakfast Strawberry and Banana Quinoa

Prep Time: 10 minutes | Cook Time: 6-8 hours | Serves: 6

1½ cups quinoa, rinsed
3 cups unsweetened cashew, coconut, or flax milk
2 cups fresh strawberries, halved, plus for more topping (optional)

1 large banana, peeled and sliced, plus more for topping (optional)
3 tablespoons almond butter or peanut butter

1. In the pot, mix together the quinoa, milk, banana, strawberries, and nut butter. Cover with the lid. 2. Turn dial to SLOW COOK, set temperature to LO, and set time to 6 hours. Cook for 6 to 8 hours until the liquid has been absorbed. 3. When cooking is complete, serve the quinoa warm, topped with additional berries or banana (if using). 4. Refrigerate leftovers for up to 1 week, or freeze for up to 1 month.

Basil Spinach Oatmeal

Prep Time: 10 minutes | Cook Time: 7-8 hours | Serves: 8

3 cups steel-cut oatmeal
2 shallots, peeled and minced
5 cups Roasted Vegetable Broth
1 cup water
1 teaspoon dried basil leaves
½ teaspoon dried thyme leaves

¼ teaspoon salt
¼ teaspoon freshly ground black pepper
½ cup grated Parmesan cheese
2 cups chopped baby spinach leaves
2 tablespoons chopped fresh basil

1. In the pot, mix the oatmeal, shallots, water, vegetable broth, basil, thyme, salt, and pepper and cover with the lid. 2. Turn dial to SLOW COOK, set temperature to LO, and set time to 7 hours. Cook for 7 to 8 hours until the oatmeal is tender. 3. Stir in the Parmesan cheese, spinach, and basil, and let stand, covered, for another 5 minutes. Stir and serve.

Delicious Eggs in Purgatory

Prep Time: 15 minutes | Cook Time: 7-8 hours | Serves: 8

2½ pounds Roma tomatoes, chopped
2 onions, chopped
2 garlic cloves, chopped
1 teaspoon paprika
½ teaspoon ground cumin

½ teaspoon dried marjoram leaves
1 cup Roasted Vegetable Broth
8 large eggs
2 red chili peppers, minced
½ cup chopped flat-leaf parsley

1. In the pot, mix the tomatoes, garlic, paprika, onions, cumin, marjoram, and vegetable broth, and stir to mix. Cover with the lid. 2. Turn dial to SLOW COOK, set temperature to LO, and set time to 7 hours. Cook for 7 to 8 hours until a sauce has formed. 3. One at a time, break the eggs into the sauce and do not stir. 4. Cover and cook on high until the egg whites are fully set and the yolk is thickened, about 20 minutes. Sprinkle the eggs with the minced red chili peppers. 5. When cooking is complete, sprinkle with the parsley and serve.

Three-Grain Granola with Nuts

Prep Time: 15 minutes | Cook Time: 3½-5 hours | Serves: 40

5 cups regular oatmeal
4 cups barley flakes
3 cups buckwheat flakes
2 cups whole almonds
2 cups whole walnuts

½ cup honey
2 teaspoons ground cinnamon
1 tablespoon vanilla extract
2 cups golden raisins
2 cups dried cherries

1. In the pot, mix the oatmeal, buckwheat flakes, barley flakes, almonds, and walnuts. 2. In a small bowl, mix the cinnamon, honey, and vanilla, and mix well. Drizzle this mixture over the food in the pot and stir with a spatula to coat. 3. Partially cover the pot with lid. Turn dial to SLOW COOK, set temperature to LO, and set time to 3½ hours. Cook for 3½ to 5 hours, stirring twice during cooking time, until the oatmeal, barley and buckwheat flakes, and nuts are toasted. 4. When cooking is complete, remove the granola from the pot and spread on two large baking sheets. Add the raisins and cherries to the granola and stir gently. 5. Let the granola cool and then store in an airtight container at room temperature.

Sweet Breakfast Cobbler

Prep Time: 15 minutes | Cook Time: 5-7 hours | Serves: 4

3 cups peeled, sliced tart apples
1 tsp cinnamon
2 cups granola cereal

¼ cup honey
3 Tbsp melted butter

1. Grease the inside of pot with nonstick cooking spray. 2. Put the apples into the pot and sprinkle with the cinnamon and granola. 3. In a separate bowl, stir together the honey and butter. Sprinkle over the apple mixture. Mix everything together gently and cover with lid. 4. Turn dial to SLOW COOK, set temperature to LO, and set time to 5 hours. Cook for 5 to 7 hours. Check for doneness with a fork. 5. When cooking is complete, serve with fruit, yogurt or ice cream, if desired.

Spinach and Feta Quiche

Prep Time: 15 minutes | Cook Time: 5-6 hours | Serves: 6

1 tablespoon extra-virgin olive oil
12 large eggs
1 cup whole-grain biscuit mix or whole-grain pancake and waffle mix
1 cup 2 percent milk

2 cups baby spinach
1½ cups crumbled feta cheese, plus more for topping (optional)
1 teaspoon garlic powder
½ teaspoon sea salt

1. Coat the bottom of pot with the olive oil. 2. Add the biscuit mix, eggs, and milk. Whisk together until smooth. 3. Add the spinach, garlic powder, cheese, and salt. Mix well and cover with lid. 4. Turn dial to SLOW COOK, set temperature to LO, and set time to 5 hours. Cook for 5 to 6 hours until the center of the quiche has set and the edges are golden brown. 5. When cooking is complete, serve the quiche with additional cheese on top, if desired. Do not top with cheese if you are in the pureed-foods stage. 6. Refrigerate any leftovers for up to 5 days, or freeze for up to 1 month.

Vanilla Zucchini-Carrot Bread

Prep Time: 15 minutes | Cook Time: 3 hours | Serves: 8

2 teaspoons butter, for greasing pan
1 cup almond flour
1 cup granulated erythritol
½ cup coconut flour
1½ teaspoons baking powder
1 teaspoon ground cinnamon
½ teaspoon ground nutmeg

½ teaspoon baking soda
¼ teaspoon salt
4 eggs
½ cup butter, melted
1 tablespoon pure vanilla extract
1½ cups finely grated zucchini
½ cup finely grated carrot

1. Lightly grease a loaf pan that fits your pot with the butter and set aside. 2. Place a small rack in the bottom of your pot. 3. In a large bowl, mix up the almond flour, erythritol, coconut flour, cinnamon, nutmeg, baking powder, baking soda, and salt until well mixed. 4. In a separate medium bowl, whisk together the melted butter, eggs, and vanilla until well blended. 5. Pour the wet ingredients into dry ingredients and stir to combine. 6. Stir in the zucchini and carrot. 7. Spoon the batter into the prepared loaf pan. 8. Put the loaf pan on the rack in the bottom of the pot and cover with lid. 9. Turn dial to SLOW COOK, set temperature to HI, and set time to 3 hours. 10. When cooking is complete, take out the loaf pan out, let the bread cool completely, and serve.

Crunchy Keto Granola

Prep Time: 10 minutes | Cook Time: 3-4 hours | Serves: 16

½ cup coconut oil, melted
2 teaspoons pure vanilla extract
1 teaspoon maple extract
1 cup chopped pecans
1 cup sunflower seeds
1 cup unsweetened shredded coconut

½ cup hazelnuts
½ cup slivered almonds
¼ cup granulated erythritol
½ teaspoon cinnamon
¼ teaspoon ground nutmeg
¼ teaspoon salt

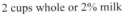

1. Lightly grease the pot with 1 tablespoon of the coconut oil. 2. In a large bowl, whisk together the remaining coconut oil, vanilla, and maple extract. Add the pecans, coconut, hazelnuts, almonds, sunflower seeds, erythritol, cinnamon, nutmeg, and salt. Toss to coat the nuts and seeds. 3. Transfer the mixture to the pot and cover with lid. 4. Turn dial to SLOW COOK, set temperature to LO, and set time to 3 hours. Cook for 3 to 4 hours until the granola is crispy. 5. When cooking is complete, transfer the granola to a baking sheet lined with parchment paper or aluminum foil to cool. 6. Store in a sealed airtight in the refrigerator for up to 2 weeks.

Apple Oatmeal

Prep Time: 20 minutes | Cook Time: 5-7 hours | Serves: 1

2 cups whole or 2% milk
¼ cup brown sugar
2 Tbsp honey
2 Tbsp melted butter
¼ tsp salt

½ tsp cinnamon
1 cup steel cut or regular oats
1 cup apples, peeled, chopped
½ cup dates, raisins, chopped
½ cup nuts to your liking, chopped

1. Grease the inside of pot with nonstick cooking spray. 2. Combine milk, honey, melted butter, brown sugar, salt, and cinnamon in the pot and mix well. 3. Mix in the oats, apples, dates or raisins, and the nuts. Cover the pot with lid. 4. Turn dial to SLOW COOK, set temperature to LO, and set time to 5 hours. Cook for 5 to 7 hours until oatmeal is tender. 5. When cooking is complete, stir well before serving.

Caramelized Peach Steel-Cut Oats

Prep Time: 10 minutes | Cook Time: 8 hours | Serves: 6-8

1 tablespoon butter, plus more for serving
2 cups steel-cut oats
2 peaches, peeled, pitted, and sliced
½ cup heavy (whipping) cream

½ cup brown sugar
1 tablespoon vanilla extract
1 teaspoon sea salt
4 cups water

1. Coat the interior of the pot with the butter, making sure to cover about two-thirds up the sides of the pot. 2. Put the oats, peaches, cream, vanilla, salt, brown sugar, and water in the pot. Stir gently to mix. 3. Cover the pot with lid. Turn dial to SLOW COOK, set temperature to LO, and set time to 8 hours. 4. When cooking is complete, serve with additional butter.

Nutty Granola with Seeds and Dried Fruit

Prep Time: 10 minutes | Cook Time: 6 hours | Serves: 10

1 overripe banana, peeled
3 tablespoons water
6 cups old-fashioned oats
½ cup chopped pecans
½ cup chopped walnuts
½ cup raw cashews
½ cup slivered or chopped raw almonds
½ cup unsweetened coconut flakes
3 tablespoons ground flaxseed

3 tablespoons raw pepitas
3 tablespoons raw sunflower seeds
3 tablespoons chia seeds
½ cup maple syrup
½ cup aquafaba
½ cup raisins
½ cup currants
½ cup unsweetened dried cherries

1. In the bottom of the pot, mash together the banana and water. Add the oats, pecans, walnuts, almonds, cashews, coconut, pepitas, flaxseed, sunflower seeds, chia seeds, and maple syrup. 2. In a small bowl, use an electric beater to whip the aquafaba into almost-stiff peaks, about 5 minutes. Add it to the pot and stir to combine. 3. To keep the condensation that forms on the inside of the lid away from the granola, stretch a clean dish towel or several layers of paper towels over the top of the pot, but not touching the food, and place the lid on top of the towel(s). 4. Turn dial to SLOW COOK, set temperature to LO, and set time to 6 hours. Cook for 6 hours, stirring every hour to make sure the granola does not burn and replacing the damp towels as needed. 5. After 6 hours, the granola will be darker in color. Transfer it to a parchment-lined baking sheet, spread it out, and let it cool for up to 1 hour. Once it's completely cool and crispy, sprinkle on the raisins, currants, and dried cherries and stir to combine. Store in a large sealed container for up to 2 weeks.

Classic Huevos Rancheros

Prep Time: 15 minutes | Cook Time: 6 hours | Serves: 6

1 tablespoon coconut oil
1 pound Mexican chorizo, casings removed
1 onion, diced
2 cups salsa
10 large eggs

1 cup ricotta cheese
2 cups grated Cheddar cheese, divided
¾ cup heavy (whipping) cream or half-and-half
1 (4-ounce) can diced green chiles, drained
½ teaspoon kosher salt

1. Remove the lid from the pot. Turn dial to SEAR/SAUTÉ, set temperature to LO, and press START/STOP to begin preheating. Let the unit preheat for 5 minutes. 2. When preheating is complete, heat the coconut oil in the pot. 3. Add the chorizo and onion and sauté until the sausage is browned and the onions are soft, about 5 minutes. 4. Stir the salsa into the sausage. 5. In a large bowl, beat the eggs, then whisk in the ricotta cheese, 1 cup of Cheddar cheese, green chiles, heavy cream, and salt. Pour the egg mixture on top of the sausage mixture in the pot. 6. Sprinkle the remaining 1 cup of Cheddar cheese over the top. Cover the pot with lid. Turn dial to SLOW COOK, set temperature to LO, and set time to 6 hours. 7. When cooking is complete, serve hot.

French Toast with Mixed Berries

Prep Time: 10 minutes | Cook Time: 2 hours | Serves: 6-8

1 tablespoon butter, plus more for serving
2 cups whole milk
6 large eggs
1 tablespoon vanilla extract
½ teaspoon ground cinnamon

1 loaf artisan white bread (see tip), cut into 2-inch pieces
2 (6-ounce) containers mixed berries, such as blueberries, raspberries, and strawberries
Maple syrup, for serving

1. Coat the interior of the pot with the butter, making sure to cover about two-thirds up the sides of the pot. 2. In a bowl, whisk together the milk, eggs, vanilla, and cinnamon. 3. Put the bread and berries in the pot and pour the egg mixture over the top. Gently tap the pot on the countertop to ensure the egg mixture settles into any air pockets. 4. Cover the pot with lid. Turn dial to SLOW COOK, set temperature to HI, and set time to 2 hours. 5. When cooking is complete, serve with additional butter and the maple syrup.

Coconut Almond and Cherry Granola

Prep Time: 10 minutes | Cook Time: 5½ hours | Serves: 6-8

5 cups old-fashioned rolled oats
1 cup slivered almonds
¼ cup mild honey
¼ cup canola oil

1 teaspoon vanilla extract
½ cup dried tart cherries
¼ cup unsweetened flaked coconut
½ cup sunflower seeds

1. Place the oats and almonds into the pot. Drizzle with honey, oil, and vanilla. Stir the mixture to distribute the syrup evenly. 2. Turn dial to SLOW COOK, set temperature to HI, and set time to 1½ hours. Cook, uncovered, stirring every 15–20 minutes. 3. Add the coconut, cherries, and sunflower seeds. 4. Set temperature to LO and cook for 4 hours, uncovered, stirring every 20 minutes. 5. When cooking is complete, allow the granola to cool fully, and then store it in an airtight container for up to 1 month.

Orange Almond Muffins

Prep Time: 15 minutes | Cook Time: 20-22 minutes | Serves: 6

1 large egg, separated
1 teaspoon extra-virgin olive oil
2 tablespoons nonfat Greek yogurt
2 teaspoons almond extract
1½ cups gluten-free oat flour
2 tablespoons wheat germ
1 teaspoon baking powder

½ teaspoon baking soda
1 teaspoon orange zest
½ cup slivered blanched almonds, divided
¼ cup low-fat buttermilk
⅓ cup orange juice
2 teaspoons light brown sugar

1. In a medium bowl, whip the egg yolk with a whisk until frothy. Add the olive oil and whisk some more. Add the Greek yogurt and almond extract while whisking. 2. In another medium bowl, mix together the oat flour, baking powder, wheat germ, baking soda, orange zest, and ¼ cup of the almonds. 3. Gently fold the egg yolk mixture into the flour mixture. 4. In another medium bowl, stir the egg whites until frothy and white. Fold it into the muffin batter. 5. Slowly add the buttermilk and orange juice, gently mixing after each addition until smooth. 6. Line a muffin tin that fits your pot with 6 paper liners and fill each liner with an equal amount of the batter. Sprinkle the top with the brown sugar and the remaining ¼ cup almonds. 7. Place the muffin tin in the pot and cover pot with lid. 8. Turn dial to BAKE, set temperature to 375°F, and set time to 20 minutes. Press START/STOP to continue cooking. Bake for 20 to 22 minutes a toothpick inserted in the center comes out clean. 9. The muffins will keep for 3 to 5 days stored in a plastic bag in the refrigerator. These also freeze well for up to a month if sealed tightly in a plastic freezer bag.

Cream Cheese Peach Casserole

Prep Time: 10 minutes | Cook Time: 6-8 hours | Serves: 6-8

1 tablespoon butter
6 cups cubed white bread
4 cups peeled, pitted, and sliced peaches
8 ounces cream cheese, cut into 1-inch pieces
12 eggs

1 cup half-and-half
¼ cup brown sugar
1 teaspoon vanilla extract
½ teaspoon sea salt

1. Coat the interior of the pot with the butter, making sure to cover about two-thirds up the sides of the pot. 2. In the pot, layer half of the bread, half of the peaches, and half of the cream cheese in that order. Repeat with the remaining bread, peaches, and cream cheese. 3. In a bowl, whisk together the eggs, half-and-half, brown sugar, vanilla, and salt. Pour the mixture into the pot. 4. Cover the pot with lid. Turn dial to SLOW COOK, set temperature to LO, and set time to 6 hours. Cook for 6 to 8 hours until the casserole is fully set. 5. When cooking is complete, let it cool for at least 10 minutes before serving.

Easy Challah French Toast Casserole

Prep Time: 10 minutes | Cook Time: 6-8 hours | Serves: 8

Nonstick spray
½ loaf day-old challah, thickly sliced
¼ cup raisins
6 eggs
1 teaspoon vanilla extract

2 cups evaporated milk
3 tablespoons granulated sugar
1 teaspoon cinnamon
¼ teaspoon nutmeg
¼ teaspoon kosher salt

1. Spray the pot with nonstick spray. Layer the challah in the pot and sprinkle with the raisins. 2. In a small bowl, whisk the eggs, vanilla, sugar, cinnamon, evaporated milk, nutmeg, and salt. Pour over the challah and raisins. 3. Cover the pot with lid. Turn dial to SLOW COOK, set temperature to LO, and set time to 6 hours. Cook for 6 to 8 hours. 4. Remove the lid and cook for 30 minutes or until the liquid has evaporated. 5. When cooking is complete, serve and enjoy.

Breakfast Quinoa with Walnuts and Apples

Prep Time: 10 minutes | Cook Time: 2 hours | Serves: 4

Nonstick spray
1 cup quinoa, rinsed well
½ cup dried apples, chopped
½ cup chopped walnuts
¼ cup maple syrup
½ teaspoon cinnamon

¼ teaspoon nutmeg
¼ teaspoon salt
1 (12-ounce) can evaporated milk (regular, low-fat, or fat-free)
½ cup water

1. Spray the inside of pot with nonstick spray. 2. Pour the quinoa into the prepared pot and stir in the apples, walnuts, cinnamon, nutmeg, maple syrup, and salt. 3. Add the milk and water to a 2-quart saucepan. Place over medium heat and heat to a bare simmer. Stir into the quinoa mixture. 4. Cover the pot with lid. Turn dial to SLOW COOK, set temperature to HI, and set time to 2 hours. 5. When cooking is complete, let sit for about 5 minutes before serving.

Fresh Tomato and Feta Frittata

Prep Time: 5 minutes | Cook Time: 6-8 hours | Serves: 8

Cooking spray
12 large eggs
1½ cups chopped fresh tomatoes
4 ounces feta cheese, crumbled
½ cup half and half

1 garlic clove, minced
1 teaspoon dried chopped onion
½ teaspoon dried basil
½ teaspoon salt
¼ teaspoon freshly ground black pepper

1. Coat the pot generously with cooking spray. 2. In a medium bowl, stir together the eggs, tomatoes, half and half, garlic, onion, basil, salt, feta, and pepper. 3. Pour the mixture into the pot. 4. Cover the pot with lid. Turn dial to SLOW COOK, set temperature to LO, and set time to 6 hours. Cook for 6 to 8 hours on low or for 3 to 4 hours on high, or until the eggs are set. 5. When cooking is complete, serve and enjoy.

Simple Cheese Omelet

Prep Time: 5 minutes | Cook Time: 6-8 hours | Serves: 8

Cooking spray
8 large eggs
½ cup low-fat 1% milk
1 pound low-fat cheese (choose a combination of three:

Cheddar, Jack, Colby, Swiss, or your favorite), shredded
½ teaspoon salt
¼ teaspoon freshly ground black pepper

1. Coat the pot generously with cooking spray. 2. In a medium bowl, whisk together the salt, eggs, milk, cheese, and pepper. Pour into the pot. 3. Cover the pot with lid. Turn dial to SLOW COOK, set temperature to LO, and set time to 6 hours. Cook for 6 to 8 hours on low or for 3 to 4 hours on high, or until the eggs are set. 4. When cooking is complete, serve and enjoy.

Crustless Quiche Lorraine

Prep Time: 10 minutes | Cook Time: 4-6 hours | Serves: 6

Cooking spray
5 large eggs
5 egg whites
8 ounces bacon, cooked and crumbled
½ cup chopped onion
1 tablespoon extra-virgin olive oil

1 cup reduced-fat 2% milk
1 cup shredded Swiss cheese
½ teaspoon salt
½ teaspoon freshly ground black pepper
½ teaspoon chives

1. Coat the pot generously with cooking spray. 2. In a large bowl, whisk together the egg whites, eggs, olive oil, milk, cheese, salt, bacon, onion, pepper, and chives. Pour into the pot. 3. Cover the pot with lid. Turn dial to SLOW COOK, set temperature to LO, and set time to 4 hours. Cook on low for 4 to 6 hours or on high for 2 to 3 hours. 5. When cooking is complete, serve and enjoy.

Buttered Cheese Grits

Prep Time: 5 minutes | Cook Time: 6-9 hours | Serves: 4

2 cups stone-ground grits
6 cups water
2 tablespoons butter
1 cup shredded Cheddar cheese

2 teaspoons kosher salt
¼ teaspoon black pepper
⅛ teaspoon cayenne pepper

1. Add all ingredients to the pot. 2. Cover the pot with lid. Turn dial to SLOW COOK, set temperature to LO, and set time to 6 hours. Cook for 6 to 9 hours. 3. When cooking is complete, serve and enjoy.

Tex-Mex Scrambled Egg

Prep Time: 10 minutes | Cook Time: 6-8 hours | Serves: 8

Cooking spray
12 large eggs
⅓ cup reduced-fat 2% milk
4 ounces Cheddar cheese, shredded
1 teaspoon salt
½ teaspoon freshly ground black pepper

1 small onion, chopped
2 bell peppers, seeded and chopped
1 jalapeño, seeded and chopped
¼ cup cherry tomatoes, sliced
⅓ cup chopped fresh cilantro

1. Coat the pot generously with cooking spray. 2. In a medium bowl, whisk together the milk, eggs, cheese, black pepper, onion, bell peppers, salt, jalapeño, tomatoes, and cilantro. 3. Pour the mixture into the pot. 4. Turn dial to SLOW COOK, set temperature to LO, and set time to 6 hours. Cook for 6 to 8 hours on low or for 3 to 4 hours on high, or until the eggs are set. 5. When cooking is complete, use a fork to "scramble" the mixture before serving.

Chapter 2 Vegetables and Sides

Slow-Cooked Drunken Beans......................23

Herbed Vegetable Broth 23

Flavorful Stuffed Sweet Potatoes 23

Lemon Garlic Asparagus...........................24

Mashed Root Vegetables...........................24

Slow-Cooked Summer Vegetables 24

Delicious Udon Noodle Soup with Vegetables ...25

Classic Harvard Beets and Onions 25

Quinoa with Brussels Sprouts and Walnuts 25

Spicy Rice-Stuffed Peppers........................26

Herbed Garlic Smashed Potatoes 26

Thai Green Curry with Tofu 26

Buffalo Cauliflower Chili 27

Cheesy Stuffed Tomatoes 27

Spaghetti Squash with Creamy Tomato Sauce ...27

Yellow Squash Casserole with Crackers...........28

Garlic Cauliflower Mashed "Potatoes" 28

Balsamic Brussels Sprouts with Cranberries 28

Buttered Cauliflower Mash..........................29

Spaghetti Squash.....................................29

Cabbage with Bacon and Pearl Onions 29

Tex-Mex Kale with Garlic Tomatoes 29

Citrus Beets...30

Slow-Cooked Cauliflower Mac and Cheese 30

Curried Squash with Garlic..........................30

Brown Sugar Glazed Carrots 30

Flavorful Mediterranean Vegetable Stew 31

Easy Braised Leeks 31

Vegan White Bean Cassoulet 31

Tasty Southern Collards 32

Zucchini Ragout with Spinach 32

Balsamic Braised Red Cabbage 32

"Creamed" Spinach...................................33

Delicious Vegetarian Stuffed Peppers..............33

Balsamic Bacon and Vegetable Medley...........33

Slow-Cooked Drunken Beans

Prep Time: 10 minutes | Cook Time: 7-9 hours | Serves: 8

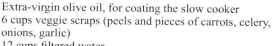

1½ pounds dried pinto beans
3 strips bacon
1 onion, chopped
3 cloves garlic, minced
1 (12-ounce) bottle beer
6 cups water

1 (4-ounce) can diced green chiles
2 cups chunky salsa
1 teaspoon salt
⅛ teaspoon pepper
½ cup chopped cilantro

1. Sort through beans and rinse thoroughly. Cover with water and let soak overnight. 2. Remove the lid from the pot. Turn dial to SEAR/SAUTÉ, set temperature to LO, and press START/STOP to begin preheating. Let the unit preheat for 5 minutes. 3. When preheating is complete, fry bacon until crisp. Drain on paper towels, crumble, and refrigerate. 4. Cook onions and garlic in bacon drippings until crisp and tender, and set aside. 5. Drain beans and add to the pot along with onion mixture, beer, and water. Cover with the lid. 6. Turn dial to SLOW COOK, set temperature to LO, and set time to 6 hours. Cook for 6 to 7 hours until beans are tender. 7. Stir beans and add chiles, salt, salsa, and pepper. Cover again and cook for 1 to 2 hours longer until beans are very tender. Sprinkle with cilantro and reserved bacon pieces, stir, and serve.

Herbed Vegetable Broth

Prep Time: 15 minutes | Cook Time: 6-8 hours | Serves: 12

Extra-virgin olive oil, for coating the slow cooker
6 cups veggie scraps (peels and pieces of carrots, celery, onions, garlic)
12 cups filtered water
½ medium onion, roughly chopped
2 garlic cloves, roughly chopped

1 parsley sprig
¾ teaspoon sea salt
½ teaspoon dried oregano
½ teaspoon dried basil leaves
2 bay leaves

1. Coat the pot with a thin layer of olive oil. 2. In the pot, combine the veggie scraps, onion, water, garlic, parsley, salt, oregano, basil, and bay leaves. Cover the pot with lid. 3. Turn dial to SLOW COOK, set temperature to LO, and set time to 6 hours. Cook for 6 to 8 hours. 4. Pour the cooked broth through a fine-mesh sieve set over a large bowl, discarding the veggie scraps. Refrigerate the broth in airtight containers for up to 5 days, or freeze for up to 3 months.

Flavorful Stuffed Sweet Potatoes

Prep Time: 15 minutes | Cook Time: 6-7 hours | Serves: 4

4 medium sweet potatoes
1 cup Hatch Chile "Refried" Beans

4 tablespoons chopped scallions (both white and green parts)
1 avocado, peeled, pitted, and quartered

1. Wash the sweet potatoes, but do not dry them. The water left on the skins from washing is the only moisture needed for cooking. Put the damp sweet potatoes in the pot and cover with the lid. 2. Turn dial to SLOW COOK, set temperature to LO, and set time to 6 hours. Cook for 6 to 7 hours. A fork should easily poke through when they are done. 3. When cooking is done, carefully remove the hot sweet potatoes from the pot. Slice each one lengthwise about halfway through. Mash the revealed flesh with a fork, and fill the opening with ¼ cup of beans. Top each with 1 tablespoon of scallions and a quarter of the avocado and serve.

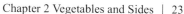

Lemon Garlic Asparagus

Prep Time: 10 minutes | Cook Time: 4-6 hours | Serves: 4

2 pounds asparagus, ends trimmed
Juice of 2 lemons (4 to 6 tablespoons)
½ cup low-sodium chicken broth or water
2 garlic cloves, minced
1 teaspoon basil

1 teaspoon garlic salt
½ teaspoon freshly ground black pepper
¼ teaspoon red pepper flakes
1 lemon, sliced

1. Place the asparagus in the bottom of the pot. 2. In a small bowl, stir together the lemon juice, broth, garlic salt, garlic, basil, black pepper, and red pepper flakes. 3. Pour the sauce over the asparagus, then top with the lemon slices. 4. Cover the pot with lid. Turn dial to SLOW COOK, set temperature to LO, and set time to 4 hours. Cook on low for 4 to 6 hours or on high for 2 to 3 hours. 5. When cooking is complete, serve and enjoy.

Mashed Root Vegetables

Prep Time: 15 minutes | Cook Time: 6-7 hours | Serves: 6-8

1 tablespoon butter
1 tablespoon extra-virgin olive oil
2 tablespoons minced garlic
1 teaspoon sea salt
½ teaspoon ground black pepper
1½ teaspoons dried thyme
2 pounds mixed root vegetables (any combination of sweet

potatoes, white potatoes, carrots, turnips, and parsnips),
peeled and chopped
¼ cup Savory Vegetable Broth or store-bought vegetable
broth
⅓ cup 2 percent milk, whole milk, or half-and-half
Sliced scallions, for topping (optional)
¾ to 1 cup sour cream, for topping (optional)

1. In the pot, combine the butter, olive oil, salt, garlic, black pepper, and thyme. 2. Turn dial to SLOW COOK, set temperature to HI, and set time to 2 minutes. Cook for 2 to 3 minutes, stirring frequently, until fragrant. 3. Add the root vegetables, broth, and milk. Mix well and cover with the lid. 4. Set the temperature to LO and cook for 6 to 7 hours, starting checking for doneness after 6 hours, until the root vegetables are easily mashed. 5. When cooking is done, turn off the pot. Either transfer the contents to a large mixing bowl and mash coarsely using a hand masher, or transfer to a blender and puree. 6. Serve the vegetables warm, topped with scallions if using, and 2 tablespoons of sour cream per serving if using. Do not use the scallions if you are at the pureed-foods stage. 7. Refrigerate leftovers for up to 5 days, or freeze for up to 1 month.

Slow-Cooked Summer Vegetables

Prep Time: 15 minutes | Cook Time: 4-5 hours | Serves: 6-8

½ cup extra-virgin olive oil
½ cup balsamic vinegar
2 tablespoons chopped fresh basil leaves
1 tablespoon dried thyme
1 (16-ounce) can chopped or diced tomatoes, drained

1 cup chopped white onion
2½ cups sliced or chopped cored orange and yellow bell
peppers
3 cups sliced peeled zucchini

1. In the pot, combine the olive oil, basil, vinegar, and thyme. Turn dial to SLOW COOK, set temperature to HI, and set time to 2 minutes. Cook for 2 to 3 minutes, stirring frequently, until fragrant. 2. Add the tomatoes, onion, bell peppers, and zucchini. Mix well and cover with the lid. 3. Set the temperature to LO and cook for 4 to 5 hours until the vegetables are soft. 4. When cooking is done, turn off the pot. Serve the vegetables warm on their own or as a side dish. 5. Refrigerate the leftovers for up to 3 days, or freeze for up to 1 month.

Delicious Udon Noodle Soup with Vegetables

Prep Time: 15 minutes | Cook Time: 6 hours | Serves: 4

2 tablespoons extra-virgin olive oil
2 scallions, both white and green parts, chopped
1 tablespoon chopped peeled fresh ginger
2 tablespoons minced garlic
1 cup sliced shiitake mushrooms
2 tablespoons low-sodium soy sauce or coconut aminos

6 cups Savory Vegetable Broth or store-bought vegetable broth
2 teaspoons red or white miso
1 cup chopped bok choy
8 to 10 ounces dried udon
Fresh spinach and shredded carrots, for topping (optional)

1. In the pot, combine the olive oil, scallions, ginger, garlic, mushrooms, and soy sauce. 2. Turn dial to SLOW COOK, set temperature to HI, and set time to 2 minutes. Cook for 2 to 3 minutes, stirring frequently, until fragrant. 3. Pour in the broth and stir. 4. Add the miso and stir until dissolved. 5. Add the bok choy and udon. Mix thoroughly, making sure the udon is fully submerged, and cover with the lid. 6. Cook on low for 6 hours until the udon is cooked. 7. When cooking is done, turn off the pot. Serve the noodle soup warm over a handful of fresh spinach if using, and a handful of shredded carrots if using. Do not add the carrots if you are in the soft-foods stage. 8. Refrigerate the leftovers for up to 1 week, or freeze for up to 2 months.

Classic Harvard Beets and Onions

Prep Time: 20 minutes | Cook Time: 5-7 hours | Serves: 8

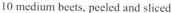

10 medium beets, peeled and sliced
3 red onions, chopped
4 garlic cloves, minced
⅓ cup honey
⅓ cup lemon juice

1 cup water
2 tablespoons melted coconut oil
3 tablespoons cornstarch
½ teaspoon salt

1. In the pot, mix the beets, onions, and garlic. 2. In a medium bowl, mix the honey, lemon juice, water, cornstarch, coconut oil, and salt until well combined. Pour this mixture over the beets and cover with lid. 3. Turn dial to SLOW COOK, set temperature to LO, and set time to 5 hours. Cook for 5 to 7 hours until the beets are tender and the sauce has thickened. 4. When cooking is complete, serve.

Quinoa with Brussels Sprouts and Walnuts

Prep Time: 20 minutes | Cook Time: 5-6 hours | Serves: 8

2 cups quinoa, rinsed
1 onion, finely chopped
3 garlic cloves, minced
4 cups Roasted Vegetable Broth
3 cups Brussels sprouts

1 teaspoon dried marjoram leaves
2 tablespoons lemon juice
2 avocados, peeled and sliced
½ cup pomegranate seeds
1 cup broken walnuts

1. In the pot, mix the quinoa, onion, garlic, Brussels sprouts, vegetable broth, marjoram, and lemon juice. Cover with the lid. 2. Turn dial to SLOW COOK, set temperature to LO, and set time to 5 hours. Cook for 5 to 6 hours until the quinoa is tender. 3. When cooking is complete, top with the avocados, pomegranate seeds, and walnuts, and serve.

Spicy Rice-Stuffed Peppers

Prep Time: 10 minutes | Cook Time: 6 hours | Serves: 4

4 large bell peppers of uniform size
½ teaspoon ground chipotle pepper
¼ teaspoon hot Mexican chili powder
¼ teaspoon black pepper
½ teaspoon kosher salt

1 (15-ounce) can fire-roasted diced tomatoes with garlic
1 cup cooked long-grain rice
1½ cups broccoli florets
¼ cup finely diced onion
½ cup water

1. Cut the tops off of each pepper to form a cap. Remove the seeds from the cap. Remove the seeds and most of the ribs from inside the pepper. 2. Place the peppers, open side up, in the pot. 3. In a medium bowl, mix the spices, rice, broccoli, tomatoes, and onion. Spoon the mixture into each pepper until it is filled to the top. Replace the cap. 4. Pour the water into the bottom of the pot. 5. Cover the pot with lid. Turn dial to SLOW COOK, set temperature to LO, and set time to 6 hours. 6. When cooking is complete, serve and enjoy.

Herbed Garlic Smashed Potatoes

Prep Time: 20 minutes | Cook Time: 5-6 hours | Serves: 6

3½ pounds red or creamer potatoes, rinsed
2 onions, minced
12 garlic cloves, peeled and sliced
½ cup Roasted Vegetable Broth
3 tablespoons olive oil

1 teaspoon dried thyme leaves
1 teaspoon dried dill leaves
½ teaspoon salt
⅓ cup grated Parmesan cheese

1. In the pot, mix the potatoes, garlic, onions, vegetable broth, olive oil, thyme, dill, and salt. 2. Cover with the lid. Turn dial to SLOW COOK, set temperature to LO, and set time to 5 hours. Cook for 5 to 6 hours until the potatoes are tender. 3. Mash the potatoes in the pot with a potato masher, leaving some chunky pieces. Stir in the Parmesan cheese and serve.

Thai Green Curry with Tofu

Prep Time: 15 minutes | Cook Time: 7 hours | Serves: 4

2 tablespoons coconut oil
½ onion, diced
1 tablespoon minced fresh ginger
2 garlic cloves, minced
1 pound firm tofu, diced
½ green bell pepper, seeded and sliced

1 (14-ounce) can coconut milk
¼ cup Thai green curry paste
1 tablespoon erythritol
1 teaspoon kosher salt
½ teaspoon turmeric
¼ cup chopped fresh cilantro, for garnish

1. Remove the lid from the pot. Turn dial to SEAR/SAUTÉ, set temperature to HI, and press START/STOP to begin preheating. Let the unit preheat for 5 minutes. 2. When preheating is complete, heat the coconut oil in the pot. 3. Add the onion and sauté for about 5 minutes until softened. 4. Stir in the ginger and garlic. 5. Mix in the tofu, green bell pepper, coconut milk, erythritol, salt, curry paste, and turmeric. 6. Cover the pot with lid. Turn dial to SLOW COOK, set temperature to LO, and set time to 7 hours. 7. When cooking is complete, serve hot, garnished with the cilantro.

Buffalo Cauliflower Chili

Prep Time: 10 minutes | Cook Time: 6 hours | Serves: 4

2 tablespoons coconut oil
2 cups cauliflower florets
8 ounces firm tofu, cut into 1-inch cubes
½ onion, diced
2 cups crumbled blue cheese, divided
1 cup diced tomatoes, with juice

¼ cup all-natural spicy hot sauce (such as Frank's redhot)
1 tablespoon erythritol
1½ teaspoons chili powder
1 teaspoon ground cumin
¼ teaspoon kosher salt
2 celery stalks, finely diced

1. In the pot, combine the coconut oil, tofu, onion, 1 cup of blue cheese, tomatoes and their juice, hot sauce, erythritol, cauliflower, chili powder, cumin, and salt. Stir to mix. 2. Cover the pot with lid. Turn dial to SLOW COOK, set temperature to LO, and set time to 6 hours. 3. When cooking is complete, serve the chili hot, topped with the celery and remaining 1 cup of blue cheese.

Cheesy Stuffed Tomatoes

Prep Time: 20 minutes | Cook Time: 6-7 hours | Serves: 6

6 large tomatoes
1 red onion, finely chopped
1 yellow bell pepper, stemmed, seeded, and chopped
3 garlic cloves, minced
¾ cup low-sodium whole-wheat bread crumbs

1½ cups shredded Colby cheese
¼ cup finely chopped flat-leaf parsley
1 teaspoon dried thyme leaves
½ cup Roasted Vegetable Broth

1. Cut the tops off the tomatoes. With a serrated spoon, core the tomatoes, reserving the pulp. Set the tomatoes aside. 2. In a medium bowl, mix the onion, bell pepper, bread crumbs, garlic, cheese, parsley, thyme, and reserved tomato pulp. 3. Stuff this mixture into the tomatoes and place the tomatoes in the pot. Add the vegetable broth into the bottom of the pot and cover with the lid. 4. Turn dial to SLOW COOK, set temperature to LO, and set time to 6 hours. Cook for 6 to 7 hours until the tomatoes are tender. 5. When cooking is complete, serve.

Spaghetti Squash with Creamy Tomato Sauce

Prep Time: 10 minutes | Cook Time: 7 hours | Serves: 4

1 tablespoon coconut oil
1 small spaghetti squash, halved, seeds and pulp removed
12 ounces firm tofu, finely diced
1 (14.5-ounce) can diced tomatoes
8 ounces cream cheese, at room temperature
½ onion, diced

4 garlic cloves, minced
1 teaspoon dried oregano
¾ teaspoon kosher salt
½ teaspoon freshly ground black pepper
2 tablespoons unsalted butter
1 cup grated Parmesan cheese, divided

1. Coat the bottom of the pot with the coconut oil. 2. Place the spaghetti squash halves, cut-side down, in the bottom of the pot. 3. In a large bowl, stir together the tofu, tomatoes, cream cheese, onion, garlic, salt, oregano, and pepper. Pour the mixture into the pot, around the squash. 4. Cover the pot with lid. Turn dial to SLOW COOK, set temperature to LO, and set time to 7 hours. 5. Using tongs, carefully remove the spaghetti squash from the pot. With a fork, shred the flesh into a colander. Let the strands drain for a few minutes and then transfer to a bowl and toss with the butter. 6. To serve, divide the squash among four serving plates, top with some tomato sauce, and garnish with the Parmesan cheese.

Yellow Squash Casserole with Crackers
Prep Time: 10 minutes | Cook Time: 6 hours | Serves: 8

2 lb yellow squash, sliced across
1 cup chopped onion
2 cups salted crackers, crumbled

1 cup Cheddar cheese, shredded
1 Tbsp butter

1. Microwave the squash, onion and 1 tablespoon butter for 10 minutes uncovered. 2. Add the squash mixture together with ½ cup cheese and 1 cup cracker crumbs into the pot. 3. In a separate bowl, mix the remaining cheese and 1 cup of cracker crumbs, and sprinkle over the squash. 4. Cover with lid. Turn dial to SLOW COOK, set temperature to LO, and set time to 2 hours. 5. When cooking is complete, let stand for 30 minutes.

Garlic Cauliflower Mashed "Potatoes"
Prep Time: 5 minutes | Cook Time: 4-6 hours | Serves: 6

1 head of cauliflower
3 cups water
4 garlic cloves
1 shallot
1 bay leaf

1 tablespoon extra-virgin olive oil
1 to 2 tablespoons milk
Freshly ground black pepper
¼ cup minced chives, for garnish

1. Cut the cauliflower into florets and place them in the pot. 2. Add the water, garlic, shallot, and bay leaf. 3. Cover the pot with lid. Turn dial to SLOW COOK, set temperature to LO, and set time to 4 hours. Cook on low for 4 to 6 hours or on high for 2 to 3 hours. 4. Drain the water. Remove and discard the garlic cloves, shallot, and bay leaf. 5. Mix in the olive oil. 6. Using a potato masher, mash the cauliflower, or use an immersion blender to make it creamier. Add the milk, a little at a time, until the desired consistency is reached. 7. Season with the black pepper, and serve topped with chives. 8. Store the mashed cauliflower in an airtight, covered container in the refrigerator for 3 to 5 days. Mashed cauliflower freezes well and heats up quickly. Freeze in heavy-duty freezer bags for up to 10 months.

Balsamic Brussels Sprouts with Cranberries
Prep Time: 10 minutes | Cook Time: 4½ hours | Serves: 4

1 tablespoon stone-ground mustard
1 tablespoon extra-virgin olive oil
¼ cup water
1 pound Brussels sprouts, trimmed and halved
4 garlic cloves

⅓ cup dried cranberries, chopped
⅛ teaspoon freshly ground black pepper
Pinch paprika
½ cup balsamic vinegar

1. In a medium bowl, combine and thoroughly whisk the mustard, olive oil, and water. 2. In the pot, place the Brussels sprouts, garlic, and dried cranberries. Add the mustard dressing and stir to coat. Season with the black pepper, salt, and paprika. 3. Turn dial to SLOW COOK, set temperature to LO, and set time to 4½ hours. Cook on low for 4½ hours or on high for 2 hours and 15 minutes, or until sprouts are tender and lightly browned. 4. Add the vinegar to another small pot and bring to a boil. Reduce to a simmer and cook, stirring frequently, until it thickens to a syrup-like consistency, about 12 minutes. 5. When cooking is complete, stir the sprouts and drizzle with the balsamic reduction. Serve immediately. 6. The cooked Brussels sprouts will keep in the refrigerator, stored in an airtight container, for 3 to 5 days. You can also freeze them in heavy-duty freezer bags for up to 10 months.

Buttered Cauliflower Mash

Prep Time: 5 minutes | Cook Time: 2-3 hours | Serves: 6-8

1 large head cauliflower, cut into 2-inch pieces
½ cup Low-Sodium Chicken Broth, or store-bought
1 garlic clove, peeled and smashed

8 tablespoons (1 stick) unsalted butter, cut into pieces
½ teaspoon sea salt

1. Put the cauliflower, garlic, butter, salt, and chicken broth in the pot. Stir to mix. 2. Cover the pot with lid. Turn dial to SLOW COOK, set temperature to LO, and set time to 2 hours. Cook on low for 2 to 3 hours or on high for 1 hour, until the cauliflower is tender. 3. When cooking is complete, using a potato masher or an immersion stick blender, mash the cauliflower until it's mostly free of lumps. Taste, and adjust the seasoning, if desired.

Spaghetti Squash

Prep Time: 15 minutes | Cook Time: 8 hours | Serves: 4-6

1 spaghetti squash, washed well

2 cups water

1. Using a fork, poke 10 to 15 holes all around the outside of the spaghetti squash. Put the squash and the water in your pot. Cover the pot with lid. 2. Turn dial to SLOW COOK, set temperature to LO, and set time to 8 hours. 3. Transfer the squash from the pot to a cutting board. Let sit for 15 minutes to cool. 4. Halve the squash lengthwise. Scrape the seeds out of the center of the squash with a spoon. Then, using a fork, scrape at the flesh until it shreds into a spaghetti-like texture. Serve warm.

Cabbage with Bacon and Pearl Onions

Prep Time: 10 minutes | Cook Time: 6 hours | Serves: 8

1 small head of cabbage, cored, chopped
⅔ cup cooked, crumbled bacon
15 oz pearl onions,

8 cups chicken broth
Salt, pepper to taste

1. Place the chopped cabbage into the pot. 2. Top with onions and bacon. Season with pepper and salt. Pour the broth over the cabbage and cover with lid. 3. Turn dial to SLOW COOK, set temperature to HI, and set time to 6 hours. 4. When cooking is complete, serve.

Tex-Mex Kale with Garlic Tomatoes

Prep Time: 20 minutes | Cook Time: 4-5 hours | Serves: 8

4 bunches kale, washed, stemmed, and cut into large pieces
2 onions, chopped
8 garlic cloves, minced
2 jalapeño peppers, minced

4 large tomatoes, seeded and chopped
1 tablespoon chili powder
½ teaspoon salt
⅛ teaspoon freshly ground black pepper

1. In the pot, mix the kale, onions, jalapeño peppers, garlic, and tomatoes. 2. Sprinkle with the salt, chili powder, and pepper, and stir to mix. 3. Cover with the lid. Turn dial to SLOW COOK, set temperature to LO, and set time to 4 hours. Cook for 4 to 5 hours until the kale is wilted and tender. 4. When cooking is complete, serve.

Citrus Beets

Prep Time: 10 minutes | Cook Time: 4 hours | Serves: 4

12 baby beets, halved, ends trimmed
1 cup orange juice
Juice of ½ lime

¼ red onion, sliced
½ teaspoon pepper

1. Add all ingredients to the pot. 2. Cover the pot with lid. Turn dial to SLOW COOK, set temperature to LO, and set time to 4 hours. 5. When cooking is complete, serve and enjoy.

Slow-Cooked Cauliflower Mac and Cheese

Prep Time: 10 minutes | Cook Time: 4-6 hours | Serves: 6

Cooking spray
2 medium heads cauliflower, cut into small florets

1 small onion, diced
3 cups Cheese Sauce

1. Coat the pot generously with cooking spray. 2. Add the cauliflower and onion to the pot. 3. Add the cheese sauce over the top. 4. Cover the pot with lid. Turn dial to SLOW COOK, set temperature to LO, and set time to 4 hours. Cook on low for 4 to 6 hours or on high for 2 to 3 hours, or until the cauliflower is tender. 5. When cooking is complete, serve and enjoy.

Curried Squash with Garlic

Prep Time: 20 minutes | Cook Time: 6-7 hours | Serves: 8

1 large butternut squash, peeled, seeded, and cut into 1-inch pieces
3 acorn squash, peeled, seeded, and cut into 1-inch pieces
2 onions, finely chopped
½ teaspoon salt

5 garlic cloves, minced
1 tablespoon curry powder
⅓ cup freshly squeezed orange juice

1. In the pot, mix all of the ingredients and cover with the lid. 2. Turn dial to SLOW COOK, set temperature to LO, and set time to 6 hours. Cook for 6 to 7 hours until squash is tender when pierced with a fork. 3. When cooking is complete, serve.

Brown Sugar Glazed Carrots

Prep Time: 10 minutes | Cook Time: 4-6 hours | Serves: 6-8

¼ cup brown sugar
½ cup orange juice
2 sage sprigs, minced

2 pounds carrots
Sea salt
8 tablespoons (1 stick) butter, cut into pieces

1. In the pot, whisk together the brown sugar and orange juice. Add the sage and carrots. Toss gently to coat them in the orange juice mixture. Season the carrots generously with salt. 2. Cover the pot with lid. Turn dial to SLOW COOK, set temperature to LO, and set time to 4 hours. Cook on low for 4 to 6 hours or on high for 2 hours, until the carrots are very tender. Add the butter during the last 10 minutes of cooking. 3. When cooking is complete, serve and enjoy.

Flavorful Mediterranean Vegetable Stew

Prep Time: 10 minutes | Cook Time: 4-6 hours | Serves: 6

2 tablespoons extra-virgin olive oil
4 garlic cloves, chopped
1 red onion, chopped
1 red bell pepper, seeded and chopped
1 eggplant, chopped
1 (15-ounce) can artichokes, drained and chopped
⅓ cup kalamata olives, pitted and chopped

2 (15-ounce) cans diced tomatoes
4 cups Vegetable Broth
1 teaspoon red pepper flakes
½ teaspoon dried oregano
½ teaspoon dried parsley
1 teaspoon salt
½ teaspoon pepper

1. In the pot, add all ingredients. 2. Cover the pot with lid. Turn dial to SLOW COOK, set temperature to LO, and set time to 4 hours. Cook for 4 to 6 hours. 3. When cooking is complete, serve and enjoy.

Easy Braised Leeks

Prep Time: 10 minutes | Cook Time: 4 hours | Serves: 6-8

4 to 6 leeks
¼ cup extra-virgin olive oil
½ cup dry white wine

Sea salt
Freshly ground black pepper

1. Cut the dark green ends from the leeks and save for another purpose. You should have about 6 to 8 inches remaining. Cut the leeks in half lengthwise and rinse them under cool running water, peeling aside the layers to wash away any trapped sediment. 2. Arrange the leeks in the pot, then add the olive oil and white wine. Season generously with the black pepper and salt. 3. Cover the pot with lid. Turn dial to SLOW COOK, set temperature to LO, and set time to 4 hours. Cook until the leeks are very tender. 4. When cooking is complete, serve and enjoy.

Vegan White Bean Cassoulet

Prep Time: 10 minutes | Cook Time: 8-10 hours | Serves: 8

1 pound dried cannellini beans
2 cups boiling water
1 ounce dried porcini mushrooms
2 leeks, sliced
1 teaspoon canola oil
2 parsnips, diced
2 carrots, diced
2 stalks celery, diced

½ teaspoon ground fennel
1 teaspoon crushed rosemary
1 teaspoon dried chervil
⅛ teaspoon cloves
¼ teaspoon salt
¼ teaspoon freshly ground black pepper
2 cups Vegetable Broth

1. The night before making the soup, place the beans in the pot. Fill with water to 1" below the top of the pot. Soak overnight. 2. Drain the beans and return them to the pot. 3. In a heat-proof bowl, pour the 2 cups of boiling water over the dried mushrooms and let them soak for 15 minutes. 4. Slice only the white and light green parts of the leeks into ¼" rounds. Cut the rounds in half. 5. In a nonstick skillet, heat the oil. Add the parsnip, celery, carrots, and leeks. Sauté for 1 minute, just until the color of the vegetables brightens. 6. Add the vegetables to the pot along with the spices. Add the mushrooms, their soaking liquid, and the broth, and stir. 7. Cover the pot with lid. Turn dial to SLOW COOK, set temperature to LO, and set time to 8 hours. Cook for 8 to 10 hours. 8. When cooking is complete, serve and enjoy.

Tasty Southern Collards

Prep Time: 10 minutes | Cook Time: 3-4 hours | Serves: 6-8

3 bunches collard greens, tough stems removed
1 teaspoon minced garlic
1 cup Vegetable Broth, or store-bought
2 tablespoons canola oil

2 tablespoons apple cider vinegar
1 tablespoon smoked paprika
1 teaspoon sea salt
¼ teaspoon red pepper flakes

1. Roll each of the collard greens into a tight cylinder and cut them into thin shreds. 2. Put the collards into the pot with the garlic, vegetable broth, oil, paprika, salt, vinegar, and red pepper flakes. Stir to mix. 3. Cover the pot with lid. Turn dial to SLOW COOK, set temperature to LO, and set time to 3 hours. Cook on low for 3 to 4 hours or on high for 1 hour 30 minutes to 2 hours, or until the greens are tender. 4. When cooking is complete, serve and enjoy.

Zucchini Ragout with Spinach

Prep Time: 10 minutes | Cook Time: 4 hours | Serves: 6

5 ounces fresh spinach
3 zucchini, diced
½ cup diced red onion
2 stalks celery, diced
2 carrots, diced
1 parsnip, diced
3 tablespoons tomato paste

¼ cup water
1 teaspoon freshly ground black pepper
¼ teaspoon kosher salt
1 tablespoon minced fresh basil
1 tablespoon minced fresh Italian parsley
1 tablespoon minced fresh oregano

1. Place all ingredients into the pot. Stir. 2. Cover the pot with lid. Turn dial to SLOW COOK, set temperature to LO, and set time to 4 hours. 3. When cooking is complete, stir before serving.

Balsamic Braised Red Cabbage

Prep Time: 10 minutes | Cook Time: 4-6 hours | Serves: 6-8

1 small head red cabbage
1 cup Vegetable Broth, or store-bought
¼ cup extra-virgin olive oil
2 tablespoons balsamic vinegar

2 teaspoons Dijon mustard
1 teaspoon smoked paprika
½ teaspoon sea salt
¼ teaspoon freshly ground black pepper

1. Cut the cabbage into 8 wedges, cutting away the core just enough to remove it while leaving the wedges as intact as possible. It's okay if some separate. Place in the pot. 2. In a bowl, stir together the vegetable broth, olive oil, vinegar, mustard, salt, paprika, and black pepper, then pour the mixture over the cabbage. 3. Cover the pot with lid. Turn dial to SLOW COOK, set temperature to LO, and set time to 4 hours. Cook on low for 4 to 6 hours or on high for 2 hours and 30 minutes, or until the cabbage is tender. 4. When cooking is complete, serve and enjoy.

"Creamed" Spinach

Prep Time: 10 minutes | Cook Time: 1-2 hours | Serves: 6

1 tablespoon margarine
1 clove garlic, minced
1 tablespoon flour
1 cup unsweetened rice milk or soymilk
½ teaspoon salt

½ teaspoon crushed red pepper
½ teaspoon dried sage
2 (12-ounce) packages frozen spinach, thawed and drained well

1. Remove the lid from the pot. Turn dial to SEAR/SAUTÉ, set temperature to LO, and press START/STOP to begin preheating. Let the unit preheat for 5 minutes. 2. When preheating is complete, melt the margarine in the pot. Add the garlic and sauté for 2 minutes before stirring in the flour. 3. Slowly pour in the rice milk or soymilk and whisk until all lumps are removed. 4. Add all remaining ingredients and stir. 5. Cover the pot with lid. Turn dial to SLOW COOK, set temperature to LO, and set time to 1 hour. Cook for 1 to 2 hours. When cooking is complete, if desired, purée with an immersion blender before serving.

Delicious Vegetarian Stuffed Peppers

Prep Time: 10 minutes | Cook Time: 4-6 hours | Serves: 4

Cooking spray
¼ cup water
¾ cup riced cauliflower
1 (15-ounce) can low-sodium crushed tomatoes
1 garlic clove, minced
¼ cup grated Parmesan cheese

1 tablespoon oregano
1 teaspoon basil
½ teaspoon salt
½ teaspoon freshly ground black pepper
4 bell peppers

1. Coat the pot generously with cooking spray. 2. Pour the water into the pot. 3. In a large bowl, mix together the cauliflower, garlic, Parmesan, oregano, basil, salt, tomatoes, and pepper. 4. Cut off the tops of the peppers and clean out the ribs and seeds. 5. Spoon ¼ of the filling into each pepper cavity. 6. Place the bell peppers in the pot. 7. Cover the pot with lid. Turn dial to SLOW COOK, set temperature to LO, and set time to 4 hours. Cook on low for 4 to 6 hours or on high for 2 to 3 hours. 8. When cooking is complete, serve and enjoy.

Balsamic Bacon and Vegetable Medley

Prep Time: 15 minutes | Cook Time: 4-6 hours | Serves: 4

Cooking spray
8 ounces bacon, cooked and crumbled
1 small onion, chopped
2 bell peppers, seeded and chopped
3 ounces carrots, peeled and chopped
3 ounces green beans, cut into 1-inch pieces

3 ounces Brussels sprouts, trimmed and halved
3 ounces beets, peeled and chopped
3 ounces summer squash or zucchini, chopped
¼ cup water
1 tablespoon extra-virgin olive oil
2 tablespoons balsamic vinegar

1. Coat the pot generously with cooking spray. 2. Add the bacon, onion, bell peppers, Brussels sprouts, carrots, green beans, beets, and squash to the pot. 3. In a small bowl, stir together the olive oil, water, and vinegar to make a sauce. Pour it over the top of the vegetables. 4. Cover the pot with lid. Turn dial to SLOW COOK, set temperature to LO, and set time to 4 hours. Cook on low for 4 to 6 hours or on high for 2 to 3 hours, or until Brussels sprouts are tender. 5. When cooking is complete, serve and enjoy.

Chapter 3 Beans and Grains

Slow Cooked Boston Baked Beans.................. 35

Whole Grain Rigatoni with Broccoli and Peas ... 35

Homemade Southwestern Veggie Bowl 35

One-Pot Chicken and Rice 36

Perfect Wild Mushroom Risotto 36

Best Cauliflower Fried Rice 36

Spicy Italian Chickpeas 37

Sweet and Spicy Chickpeas with Potatoes 37

Garlic Polenta with Fresh Vegetables 37

Comforting Parmesan Mushroom Risotto 38

Refried Pinto Beans 38

Mouthwatering Bourbon Baked Beans 38

Indian Spiced Brown Rice with Lamb 39

Mediterranean Chickpeas with Brown Rice 39

Mexican Black Beans and Brown Rice 39

Slow Cooked Boston Baked Beans
Prep Time: 10 minutes | Cook Time: 6 hours | Serves: 8

1 large sweet onion, peeled and diced
3 (15-ounce) cans cannellini, great northern, or navy beans, drained and rinsed
1 cup barbecue sauce

½ cup molasses
1 teaspoon dry mustard powder
1 (1.5- to 2-ounce) package kosher beef jerky, finely chopped
Salt, to taste

1. Add all ingredients to the pot. Stir until combined. 2. Cover the pot with lid. Turn dial to SLOW COOK, set temperature to LO, and set time to 6 hours. 3. When cooking is complete, taste for seasoning and add additional salt, if needed.

Whole Grain Rigatoni with Broccoli and Peas
Prep Time: 5 minutes | Cook Time: 20 minutes | Serves: 2

4 ounces whole grain rigatoni noodles
2 cups broccoli florets
1 cup frozen green peas, thawed
2 tablespoons Parmesan cheese

2 teaspoons extra-virgin olive oil
2 teaspoons minced garlic
Freshly ground black pepper
¼ cup chopped fresh basil

1. Fill a large pot with water and bring to a boil. Add the pasta and cook until al dente, according to the package directions. Drain the pasta. 2. While the pasta is cooking, in the pot fitted with a steamer basket that fits the pot, add 1 inch of water to the pot and cover the pot with lid. 3. Turn dial to STEAM, set time to 10 minutes, and press START/STOP to begin preheating. 4. When preheating is complete, bring water to a boil. Then add the broccoli and peas and cover with the lid again. Steam until tender. 5. In a large bowl, mix the cooked pasta, peas and broccoli. Toss with the Parmesan cheese, olive oil, and garlic. Season with the black pepper. 6. Serve immediately and garnish with the fresh basil. 7. This dish can be stored in the refrigerator in airtight containers for 3 to 5 days. It can also be frozen in airtight containers or heavy-duty freezer bags for 1 to 2 months.

Homemade Southwestern Veggie Bowl
Prep Time: 10 minutes | Cook Time: 55-60 minutes | Serves: 6

2 teaspoons extra-virgin olive oil
2 cups chopped green bell pepper
1 cup chopped red onion
4 garlic cloves, minced
1 chili pepper, minced
1 cup diced sweet potato
1 cup chopped tomato
1 cup brown rice
1 cup green lentils

1 tablespoon ground cumin
½ tablespoon freshly ground black pepper
1 tablespoon red wine vinegar
2 cups no-salt-added vegetable stock
2 cups water
4 cups chopped kale leaves
1 cup cooked black beans
2 tablespoons minced fresh cilantro
4 lime wedges, for garnish

1. Remove the lid from the pot. Turn dial to SEAR/SAUTÉ, set temperature to HI, and press START/STOP to begin preheating. Let the unit preheat for 5 minutes. 2. When preheating is complete, heat the olive oil in the pot. 3. Add the bell pepper, onion, chili pepper, sweet potato, garlic, and tomato and cook until the onions begin to look translucent, 10 to 15 minutes. 4. Add the rice, lentils, black pepper, cumin, vinegar, stock, and water. Bring to a boil and reduce the heat to a simmer. 5. Cover and cook for 45 minutes. 6. Add the kale, black beans and cilantro. Stir to mix. Garnish with the lime wedges and serve. 7. You can store the leftover cooked rice and beans in the refrigerator in airtight covered containers for 3 to 4 days. The rice and beans without the kale can also be frozen in airtight containers or heavy-duty freezer bags for 4 to 6 months.

One-Pot Chicken and Rice

Prep Time: 10 minutes | Cook Time: 6 hours | Serves: 8

2 tablespoons olive oil
1 cup mushrooms, sliced
½ cup onions, sliced
2 cups white rice, uncooked
2 tablespoons margarine
2 cups water

2 cups chicken broth
1 pound boneless, skinless chicken breast, cut into ½"-thick slices
½ teaspoon kosher salt
⅛ teaspoon black pepper

1. Remove the lid from the pot. Turn dial to SEAR/SAUTÉ, set temperature to HI, and press START/STOP to begin preheating. Let the unit preheat for 5 minutes. 2. When preheating is complete, add the olive oil to the pot and sauté the mushrooms and onions until browned, about 3 to 5 minutes. 3. Place the rest of the ingredients to the pot. 4. Cover the pot with lid. Turn dial to SLOW COOK, set temperature to LO, and set time to 6 hours. 5. When cooking is complete, serve and enjoy.

Perfect Wild Mushroom Risotto

Prep Time: 10 minutes | Cook Time: 1 hour | Serves: 6

1 teaspoon olive oil
¼ cup finely diced shallot
2 cloves garlic, minced
8 ounces sliced assorted wild mushrooms

2 cups Vegetable Broth
2 cups Arborio rice
3 cups water
½ teaspoon salt

1. Remove the lid from the pot. Turn dial to SEAR/SAUTÉ, set temperature to HI, and press START/STOP to begin preheating. Let the unit preheat for 5 minutes. 2. When preheating is complete, heat the oil in the pot. Sauté the shallot, garlic, and mushrooms until soft, about 4 to 5 minutes. 3. Add ½ cup broth and the rice and cook until the liquid is fully absorbed, about 5 minutes. 4. Add the water, salt, and remaining broth. 5. Cover the pot with lid. Turn dial to SLOW COOK, set temperature to LO, and set time to 1 hour. 6. When cooking is complete, stir before serving.

Best Cauliflower Fried Rice

Prep Time: 10 minutes | Cook Time: 15-21 minutes | Serves: 2

2 cups cauliflower florets (one head)
1 tablespoon sesame oil, divided
1 red onion, sliced
4 garlic cloves, minced
1 tablespoon minced fresh ginger
1 small red chile, thinly sliced
1 cup frozen green peas, thawed

2 cups broccoli florets
1 large carrot, julienned
½ red bell pepper, diced
2 eggs, beaten
¼ cup low-sodium vegetable broth
2 tablespoons pumpkin seeds
2 tablespoons fresh cilantro leaves

1. Pulse the cauliflower florets in a food processor until finely chopped. 2. Remove the lid from the pot. Turn dial to SEAR/SAUTÉ, set temperature to HI, and press START/STOP to begin preheating. Let the unit preheat for 5 minutes. 3. When preheating is complete, heat ½ tablespoon of the sesame oil in the pot. 4. Add the onion, garlic, ginger, and chile, and cook, stirring, until the onion is tender, about 5 minutes. 5. Add the remaining ½ tablespoon oil, the cauliflower, peas, carrot, broccoli, and bell pepper and continue to cook, stirring frequently, for 2 to 3 minutes. 6. Add the vegetable broth. Turn dial to STEAM and set time to 6 minutes. Steam, covered, until the broth has evaporated and vegetables are tender. 7. Move the vegetables to one side, add the beaten eggs, and stir quickly and thoroughly to scramble, and then mix to combine the eggs with the vegetables. Continue to cook for 2 to 3 minutes. 8. When cooking is complete, remove from heat and serve topped with pumpkin seeds and fresh cilantro.

Spicy Italian Chickpeas
Prep Time: 5 minutes | Cook Time: 4-6 hours | Serves: 6

1 pound dry chickpeas, soaked overnight
1 (28-ounce) can no-salt-added diced tomatoes
1 onion, chopped
1 bell pepper, seeded and chopped
3 garlic cloves, minced
1 teaspoon salt

½ teaspoon freshly ground black pepper
½ teaspoon paprika
½ teaspoon dried basil
½ teaspoon dried oregano
½ teaspoon dried parsley
¼ teaspoon red pepper flakes

1. In the pot, combine the chickpeas, tomatoes and their juices, onion, garlic, salt, bell pepper, pepper, paprika, basil, oregano, parsley, and red pepper flakes. Stir to mix well. 2. Cover the pot with lid. Turn dial to SLOW COOK, set temperature to LO, and set time to 4 hours. Cook for 4 to 6 hours, or until the chickpeas are tender. 3. When cooking is complete, serve.

Sweet and Spicy Chickpeas with Potatoes
Prep Time: 5 minutes | Cook Time: 4-6 hours | Serves: 8

2 pounds dry chickpeas, soaked overnight
2 bell peppers, seeded and chopped
1 onion, chopped
1 pound potatoes, peeled and chopped
¾ cup honey

⅓ cup sriracha sauce
2 tablespoons low-sodium soy sauce or tamari
2 garlic cloves, minced
1 teaspoon dried basil

1. In the pot, combine the chickpeas, onion, bell peppers, and potatoes. 2. In a medium bowl, mix together the sriracha, honey, garlic, soy sauce, and basil. Pour the sauce into the pot and stir to mix well. 3. Cover the pot with lid. Turn dial to SLOW COOK, set temperature to LO, and set time to 4 hours. Cook for 4 to 6 hours. 4. When cooking is complete, serve.

Garlic Polenta with Fresh Vegetables
Prep Time: 10 minutes | Cook Time: 40 minutes | Serves: 4

Cooking spray
1 cup polenta
4 cups water
1 teaspoon chopped garlic
1 cup sliced mushrooms
1 cup sliced red onion

1 cup broccoli florets
1 cup sliced fresh green beans
1 cup sliced yellow squash
2 tablespoons grated Parmesan cheese
Chopped fresh basil

1. Heat the oven to 350°F. Lightly spray a 3-quart ovenproof dish with the cooking spray. 2. Combine the water, polenta, and garlic in the prepared dish. Bake uncovered for about 40 minutes until the polenta pulls away from the sides of the baking dish. The polenta should be moist. 3. While the polenta is cooking, spray the pot with cooking spray. 4. Remove the lid from the pot. Turn dial to SEAR/SAUTÉ, set temperature to HI, and press START/STOP to begin preheating. Let the unit preheat for 5 minutes. 5. When preheating is complete, add the mushrooms and onion to the pot and sauté until the vegetables are tender, about 5 minutes. When done, set aside. 6. In the pot fitted with a steamer basket that fits the pot, add 1 inch of water and cover the pot with lid. 7. Turn dial to STEAM, set time to 2 minutes, and press START/STOP to begin preheating. 8. When preheating is complete, bring water to a boil. Then add the broccoli, green beans, and squash. Cover the pot with lid and steam until the vegetables are tender-crisp, 2 to 3 minutes. 9. When the polenta is done, top with the cooked vegetables. Sprinkle with the Parmesan cheese and fresh basil. Serve immediately. 10. For best results, serve the polenta right away, as it is meant to be creamy. While you can refrigerate polenta in an airtight container for 5 to 7 days, the polenta will become firm, in which case you may consider slicing it and lightly frying it. It is not recommended to freeze polenta.

Comforting Parmesan Mushroom Risotto

Prep Time: 10 minutes | Cook Time: 1½–2 hours | Serves: 6

1 teaspoon olive oil
½ cup finely diced onion
2 cloves garlic, minced
8 ounces sliced mushrooms, any variety
2 cups Vegetable Broth
2 cups Arborio rice
2 cups water

½ cup dry white wine
½ teaspoon salt
¼ cup grated Parmesan cheese
1 tablespoon butter, softened
2 tablespoons minced parsley leaves (for garnish)
Additional ¼ cup Parmesan cheese (for garnish)

1. Remove the lid from the pot. Turn dial to SEAR/SAUTÉ, set temperature to HI, and press START/STOP to begin preheating. Let the unit preheat for 5 minutes. 2. When preheating is complete, heat the oil in the pot. Sauté the onion, garlic, and mushrooms until soft, about 4 to 5 minutes. 3. Add ½ cup broth and the rice and cook until the liquid is fully absorbed, about 5 minutes. 4. Sir in the water, wine, salt, and remaining broth. 5. Cover the pot with lid. Turn dial to SLOW COOK, set temperature to HI, and set time to 1½ hours. Cook for 1½–2 hours or until all the liquid has been absorbed. 6. When cooking is complete, stir in Parmesan cheese and butter. Sprinkle with parsley and/or additional Parmesan cheese, if desired, before serving.

Refried Pinto Beans

Prep Time: 10 minutes | Cook Time: 6-8 hours | Serves: 4

Nonstick cooking spray
½ pound dry pinto beans, soaked overnight
4½ cups water
1 small onion, peeled and quartered
1 jalapeño pepper, stemmed and quartered

2 garlic cloves, minced
½ teaspoon salt
½ teaspoon freshly ground black pepper
½ teaspoon ground cumin

1. Spray the pot generously with nonstick cooking spray. 2. In the pot, combine the beans, jalapeño, garlic, salt, water, onion, pepper, and cumin. Stir to mix well. 3. Cover the pot with lid. Turn dial to SLOW COOK, set temperature to LO, and set time to 6 hours. Cook for 6 to 8 hours until the beans are tender. 4. When cooking is complete, drain the beans through a wire strainer, reserving some of the water for mashing. 5. Using a potato masher or an immersion blender, mash the beans until they reach your desired consistency. Use some of the cooking liquid to thin out the beans, if needed, and serve.

Mouthwatering Bourbon Baked Beans

Prep Time: 10 minutes | Cook Time: 6-8 hours | Serves: 8

Nonstick cooking spray
1 pound dry great northern beans, soaked overnight
5 cups low-sodium vegetable broth
1 onion, diced
1 bell pepper, seeded and diced
2 garlic cloves, minced
3 tablespoons bourbon

½ cup maple syrup
⅓ cup Ketchup
2 teaspoons no-salt-added tomato paste
1 teaspoon ground cumin
1 teaspoon paprika
1 teaspoon salt
½ teaspoon freshly ground black pepper

1. Spray the pot generously with nonstick cooking spray. 2. In the pot, combine the beans, broth, onion, garlic, bourbon, syrup, ketchup, tomato paste, cumin, paprika, salt, bell pepper, and pepper. Stir to mix well. 3. Cover the pot with lid. Turn dial to SLOW COOK, set temperature to LO, and set time to 6 hours. Cook for 6 to 8 hours. 4. When cooking is complete, stir before serving.

Indian Spiced Brown Rice with Lamb

Prep Time: 5 minutes | Cook Time: 4-6 hours | Serves: 6

1 cup uncooked brown rice
2 cups low-sodium chicken broth
1 cup Marinara Sauce
1 onion, chopped
3 garlic cloves, minced
2 teaspoons curry powder or garam masala

2 teaspoons ground cumin
2 teaspoons ground ginger
2 teaspoons ground turmeric
1 teaspoon ground coriander
½ teaspoon ground cayenne pepper
1 pound ground lamb, cooked

1. In the pot, combine the rice, broth, garlic, curry powder, cumin, ginger, turmeric, marinara sauce, onion, coriander, and cayenne pepper. Stir to mix well. 2. Cover the pot with lid. Turn dial to SLOW COOK, set temperature to LO, and set time to 4 hours. Cook for 4 to 6 hours. 3. When cooking is complete, stir in the ground lamb and serve.

Mediterranean Chickpeas with Brown Rice

Prep Time: 10 minutes | Cook Time: 4-6 hours | Serves: 4

Nonstick cooking spray
1 (15-ounce) can chickpeas, drained and rinsed
1 cup uncooked brown rice
2½ cups low-sodium vegetable broth
3 garlic cloves, minced
Juice of 1 lemon
1 tablespoon extra-virgin olive oil
1 teaspoon dried oregano

1 teaspoon paprika
1 teaspoon ground coriander
1 teaspoon ground cumin
1 teaspoon curry powder
1 teaspoon chili powder
½ teaspoon salt
¼ teaspoon freshly ground black pepper

1. Spray the pot generously with nonstick cooking spray. 2. In the pot, combine the chickpeas, rice, broth, garlic, olive oil, oregano, paprika, coriander, cumin, curry powder, chili powder, salt, lemon juice, and pepper. Stir to mix well. 3. Cover the pot with lid. Turn dial to SLOW COOK, set temperature to LO, and set time to 4 hours. Cook for 4 to 6 hours, or until the rice is tender. 5. When cooking is complete, serve.

Mexican Black Beans and Brown Rice

Prep Time: 10 minutes | Cook Time: 4-6 hours | Serves: 6

1 pound dry black beans, soaked overnight
1 onion, sliced
1 bell pepper, seeded and diced
2 celery stalks, diced
1 garlic clove, minced
1 teaspoon ground cumin
1 teaspoon chili powder

1 teaspoon paprika
1 teaspoon salt
½ teaspoon freshly ground black pepper
½ teaspoon dried thyme
1 dried bay leaf
6 cups water
4 cups cooked brown rice, warm or room temperature

1. In the pot, combine the beans, onion, celery, garlic, cumin, chili powder, paprika, salt, bell pepper, pepper, thyme, bay leaf, and water. Stir to mix well. 2. Cover the pot with lid. Turn dial to SLOW COOK, set temperature to LO, and set time to 4 hours. Cook for 4 to 6 hours, and remove the bay leaf. 3. Stir the brown rice into the pot, stirring gently until well combined, and serve.

Chapter 3 Snacks and Appetizers

Delicious Onion Chutney 41

Honeyed Pineapple Chicken Wings 41

Perfect Mole Chicken Bites 41

Meatball Biscuits with Cheese 42

Classic Eggplant Parmigiana 42

Fresh Chipotle Ranch Chicken Pizza 42

Sweet & Sour Smoked Sausage 43

Barbecued Pinto Beans 43

Classic Eggplant Caponata 43

Sweet and Sour Turkey Meatballs 44

Asian-Style Meatballs............................. 44

Spinach Artichoke Dip 44

Fresh Fig and Ginger Spread 45

Baked Sweet Potatoes 45

Homemade Stuffed Grape Leaves 45

Slow-Cooked Cheese Dip 46

Cheesy Jalapeño Poppers 46

Sweet 'n' Spicy Snack Mix.......................... 46

Lemony Chickpea Snackers 47

Chile Cheese Dip 47

Parmesan Spaghetti Squash 47

Delicious Onion Chutney

Prep Time: 10 minutes | Cook Time: 8-10 hours | Serves: 6

8 yellow onions
2 cloves garlic, chopped
¼ cup butter
1 teaspoon seasoned salt

¼ teaspoon white pepper
½ cup brown sugar
½ cup apple cider vinegar
2 tablespoons minced fresh gingerroot

1. Peel onions and coarsely chop. Combine in the pot with garlic and butter, and cover with the lid. 2. Turn dial to SLOW COOK, set temperature to LO, and set time to 8 hours. Cook for 8 to 10 hours, stirring once during cooking time, until onions are browned and caramelized. 3. Stir in the seasoned salt, brown sugar, pepper, vinegar, and gingerroot. Cover again and cook on high for 1 to 2 hours or until mixture is blended and hot. 4. When cooking is complete, remove mixture from the pot to a large bowl. Cover loosely and let cool for 1 to 2 hours before serving over Brie or Camembert cheese. Serve with crackers and toasts for spreading.

Honeyed Pineapple Chicken Wings

Prep Time: 10 minutes | Cook Time: 6-7 hours | Serves: 6

1 pound chicken wings
2 cloves garlic, minced
1 (5-ounce) can crushed pineapple
⅛ teaspoon pepper

⅓ cup honey
3 tablespoons low-sodium soy sauce
1 tablespoon vegetable oil

1. Cut the wing tip off each chicken wing and discard tips. Place the wings on a broiler rack and broil 6-inches from heat for 3 to 4 minutes until wings start to brown. 2. Mix up all of the remaining ingredients in the pot and mix well. Add wings and stir. 3. Cover with the lid. Turn dial to SLOW COOK, set temperature to LO, and set time to 6 hours. Cook for 6 to 7 hours or until wings are tender, thoroughly cooked, and glazed. 4. When cooking is complete, serve.

Perfect Mole Chicken Bites

Prep Time: 20 minutes | Cook Time: 4-6 hours | Serves: 8

2 onions, chopped
6 garlic cloves, minced
4 large tomatoes, seeded and chopped
2 dried red chilies, crushed
1 jalapeño pepper, minced

2 tablespoons chili powder
3 tablespoons cocoa powder
2 tablespoons coconut sugar
½ cup Chicken Stock
6 (5-ounce) boneless, skinless chicken breasts

1. In the pot, mix the onions, garlic, chili peppers, tomatoes, and jalapeño peppers. 2. In a medium bowl, mix the coconut sugar, chili powder, cocoa powder, and chicken stock. 3. Cut the chicken breasts into 1-inch strips crosswise and add to the pot. Pour the chicken stock mixture over all and cover with the lid. 4. Turn dial to SLOW COOK, set temperature to LO, and set time to 4 hours. Cook on low for 4 to 6 hours, or until the chicken registers 165°F on a food thermometer. 5. When cooking is complete, serve with toothpicks or little plates and forks.

Meatball Biscuits with Cheese

Prep Time: 15 minutes | Cook Time: 25 minutes | Serves: 4

12 oz. Can of any frozen flaky biscuits
Frozen cooked meatballs, 10 pcs.
String cheese, 2 sticks

Parmesan cheese, grated
Italian seasoning, 1 Tbsp
Garlic powder, 1 tsp

1. Split the 10 biscuits and cut each meatball in half. 2. Slice each stick of string cheese into 10 pieces. 3. Place one meatball half into a biscuit half and add the string cheese piece. 4. Make the balls out of the biscuits, the dough covering the meat and the cheese. 5. Place all 20 meatballs in an ungreased round cake pan that fits your pot. Sprinkle with the Parmesan cheese, Italian seasoning, and garlic powder to your liking. 6. Place the cake pan into the pot and cover with lid. Turn dial to BAKE, set temperature to 375°F, and set time to 25 minutes. Press START/STOP to continue cooking. 7. When cooking is complete, serve.

Classic Eggplant Parmigiana

Prep Time: 15 minutes | Cook Time: 6-8 hours | Serves: 6-8

3 medium eggplants, peeled, cut in 2 inch slices
⅓ cup seasoned bread crumbs
½ cup Parmesan, grated

32 oz marinara sauce
Salt, pepper to taste

1. Using olive oil, sauté the eggplants in a large skillet until lightly brown. 2. In a separate bowl, mix the seasoned bread crumbs and grated Parmesan. 3. Layer the eggplants into the pot beginning with eggplant, next top with crumbs, then marinara sauce. Repeat layers. 4. Cover with the lid. Turn dial to SLOW COOK, set temperature to LO, and set time to 5 hours. 5. When cooking is complete, serve.

Fresh Chipotle Ranch Chicken Pizza

Prep Time: 10 minutes | Cook Time: 20 minutes | Serves: 8

2 cups Bisquick mix
8 oz pepper Jack cheese, shredded
½ cup hot water
⅓ cup chipotle ranch dressing

5 Tbsp fresh cilantro, chopped
1½ cups deli rotisserie chicken, shredded
1 cup tomato, chopped

1. Grease a pizza pan that fits your pot with cooking spray. 2. In a separate bowl, stir Bisquick mix, ¾ cup of the cheese and the hot water with a spoon until soft dough forms. Press dough evenly in the pizza pan. Place the pizza pan into the pot and cover with the lid. 3. Turn dial to BAKE, set temperature to 400°F, and set time to 8 minutes. Press START/STOP to continue cooking. 4. Spread dressing evenly over partially baked crust. Sprinkle 4 Tbsp of the cilantro and ¾ cup of the cheese on the dressing. Layer the chicken, tomato and remaining cheese. 5. Bake until the edges of the crust are golden brown. Sprinkle with the remaining fresh cilantro.

Sweet & Sour Smoked Sausage

Prep Time: 10 minutes | Cook Time: 4 hours | Serves: 4

2 lb smoked sausage
2 cans (21 ounces each) cherry pie filling

1 can (20 ounces) pineapple chunks, drained
3 Tbsp brown sugar

1. Place sausages in the pot. 2. In a separate bowl, combine the pie filling, pineapple and sugar. Pour over the sausages and cover with lid. 3. Turn dial to SLOW COOK, set temperature to LO, and set time to 4 hours. 4. When cooking is complete, serve.

Barbecued Pinto Beans

Prep Time: 15 minutes | Cook Time: 8 hours | Serves: 8

5 cups cooked pinto beans, rinsed
1 onion, finely chopped
6 garlic cloves, minced
3 jalapeño peppers, seeded and finely chopped
1 (14-ounce) can tomato sauce

¼ cup blackstrap molasses
½ teaspoon liquid smoke
2 teaspoons smoked paprika
¼ teaspoon sea salt
⅛ teaspoon cayenne pepper

1. In your pot, combine all the ingredients and cover with lid. 2. Turn dial to SLOW COOK, set temperature to LO, and set time to 8 hours. 3. When cooking is complete, serve.

Classic Eggplant Caponata

Prep Time: 10 minutes | Cook Time: 2½ hours | Serves: 8

2 (1-pound) eggplants
1 teaspoon olive oil
1 red onion, diced
4 cloves garlic, minced
1 stalk celery, diced

2 tomatoes, diced
2 tablespoons nonpareil capers
2 tablespoons toasted pine nuts
1 teaspoon red pepper flakes
¼ cup red wine vinegar

1. Pierce the eggplants with a fork. Place into the pot. 2. Cover the pot with lid. Turn dial to SLOW COOK, set temperature to HI, and set time to 2 hours. 3. When cooking is complete, allow to cool. Peel off the skin. Slice each in half and remove the seeds. Discard the skin and seeds. 4. Place the eggplant pulp in a food processor. Pulse until smooth. Set aside. 5. Remove the lid from the pot. Turn dial to SEAR/SAUTÉ, set temperature to HI, and press START/STOP to begin preheating. Let the unit preheat for 5 minutes. 6. When preheating is complete, heat the oil in the pot. Sauté the onion, garlic, and celery for about 5 minutes, or until the onion has softened. 7. Add the eggplant and tomatoes. Sauté for 3 additional minutes. 8. Add the capers, pine nuts, red pepper flakes, and vinegar, and stir. 9. Continue to cook on low for 30 minutes. 10. When cooking is complete, stir prior to serving.

Sweet and Sour Turkey Meatballs

Prep Time: 15 minutes | Cook Time: 8 hours | Serves: 6

1 pound ground turkey breast
½ cup whole-wheat bread crumbs
1 onion, grated
1 egg, beaten
1 teaspoon sea salt, divided
¼ teaspoon freshly ground black pepper

1 (8-ounce) can pineapple chunks (no sugar added), with its juice
¼ cup apple cider vinegar
2 tablespoons honey
1 tablespoon cornstarch

1. In a medium bowl, mix up the ground turkey, onion, egg, ½ teaspoon of salt, bread crumbs, and the pepper. 2. Use a small scoop to form the mixture into meatballs. Put the meatballs in your pot. 3. In a small bowl, whisk together the juice from the canned pineapple, reserving the pineapple chunks, vinegar, cornstarch, honey, and remaining ½ teaspoon of salt. 4. Add the mixture to the pot and then add the pineapple chunks. 5. Cover with the lid. Turn dial to SLOW COOK, set temperature to LO, and set time to 8 hours. 6. When cooking is complete, serve.

Asian-Style Meatballs

Prep Time: 15 minutes | Cook Time: 8 hours | Serves: 6

1 pound ground turkey
6 garlic cloves, minced
6 scallions, minced
1 tablespoon grated fresh ginger
¼ cup chopped fresh cilantro

1 egg, beaten
2 tablespoons low-sodium soy sauce
½ teaspoon sesame-chili oil
¼ cup Poultry Broth, or store bought

1. In a medium bowl, combine the scallions, garlic, ginger, cilantro, egg, soy sauce, sesame-chili oil, and ground turkey, until well mixed. 2. Using a small scoop, form the mixture into balls. Put the meatballs in the pot. Add the broth and cover with the lid. 3. Turn dial to SLOW COOK, set temperature to LO, and set time to 8 hours. 6. When cooking is complete, serve.

Spinach Artichoke Dip

Prep Time: 10 minutes | Cook Time: 2 hours | Serves: 4

Cooking spray
1 tablespoon olive oil
2 cloves garlic, minced
1½ cups part-skim ricotta cheese
½ teaspoon thyme
1 teaspoon lemon zest
½ teaspoon cayenne pepper

1 (14-ounce) can artichoke hearts, drained and chopped
1 (10-ounce) package frozen spinach, thawed and drained well
¼ cup grated Parmesan cheese
½ teaspoon salt
¼ cup shredded mozzarella

1. Spray the inside of pot with nonstick spray. 2. Heat the olive oil in a small nonstick skillet over medium heat. When the oil is hot, add the garlic and cook until fragrant and pale golden, about 1 minute. Remove the skillet from the heat and let the garlic cool while proceeding with next step. 3. In a large mixing bowl, mix the ricotta cheese, lemon zest, thyme, and cayenne pepper. 4. Add the artichokes, spinach, Parmesan, salt, and cooled garlic. Stir well to combine. 5. Transfer the artichoke mixture into the prepared pot and sprinkle evenly with the mozzarella. 6. Cover the pot with lid. Turn dial to SLOW COOK, set temperature to HI, and set time to 2 hours. 7. When cooking is complete, serve hot or warm.

Fresh Fig and Ginger Spread
Prep Time: 10 minutes | Cook Time: 2-3 hours | Serves: 25

2 pounds fresh figs
2 tablespoons minced fresh ginger
2 tablespoons lime juice

½ cup water
¾ cup sugar

1. Place all ingredients in the pot and stir. 2. Cover the pot with lid. Turn dial to SLOW COOK, set temperature to LO, and set time to 2 hours. Cook for 2 to 3 hours. 3. Remove the lid and cook for an additional 2 to 3 hours until the mixture is thickened. 4. When cooking is complete, pour into airtight containers and refrigerate for up to 6 weeks.

Baked Sweet Potatoes
Prep Time: 5 minutes | Cook Time: 6 hours | Serves: 4

4 medium sweet potatoes, scrubbed

1. Wrap each sweet potato in aluminum foil and put them on the rack in the pot. 2. Cover with the lid. Turn dial to BAKE, set temperature to 300°F, and set time to 6 hours. Press START/STOP to continue cooking. 3. When cooking is complete, unwrap to serve.

Homemade Stuffed Grape Leaves
Prep Time: 10 minutes | Cook Time: 4-6 hours | Serves: 30

1 (16-ounce) jar grape leaves (about 60 leaves)
Cooking spray, as needed
¾ pound ground beef, chicken, or veal
1 shallot, minced
¾ cup cooked brown or white rice
¼ cup minced dill
½ cup lemon juice, divided use

2 tablespoons minced parsley
1 tablespoon dried mint
1 tablespoon ground fennel
¼ teaspoon freshly ground black pepper
⅛ teaspoon salt
2 cups water

1. Prepare the grape leaves according to package instructions. Set aside. 2. Spray the pot with cooking spray. 3. Remove the lid from the pot. Turn dial to SEAR/SAUTÉ, set temperature to HI, and press START/STOP to begin preheating. Let the unit preheat for 5 minutes. 4. When preheating is complete, sauté the meat and shallot until the meat is thoroughly cooked. 5. When done, drain off any excess fat. Scrape into a large bowl and add the rice, dill, ¼ cup of the lemon juice, parsley, fennel, pepper, mint, and salt. Stir to incorporate all ingredients. 6. Place a grape leaf, stem side up, with the top of the leaf pointing away from you on a clean work surface. Arrange 1 teaspoon filling in the middle of the leaf. Fold the bottom toward the middle and then fold in the sides. Roll it toward the top to seal. Repeat with the other leaves. 7. Place the rolled grape leaves in two or three layers in the pot. Add the water and remaining lemon juice to the pot. 8. Cover the pot with lid. Turn dial to SLOW COOK, set temperature to LO, and set time to 4 hours. Cook for 4 to 6 hours. 9. When cooking is complete, serve warm or cold.

Slow-Cooked Cheese Dip

Prep Time: 20 minutes | Cook Time: 2 hours | Serves: 16

1 pound lean ground beef
1 medium onion, chopped
1 large tomato, seeded and chopped
3 medium roasted jalapeños, peeled, seeded, and chopped
1 tablespoon Taco Seasoning Mix
1 to 2 chipotles in adobo, chopped to a paste, to taste

Cooking spray
1 cup whole milk
8 ounces queso quesadilla or cream cheese, cut into 1-inch cubes
1 cup grated Monterey Jack cheese
½ cup grated Cheddar cheese

1. In a large bowl, add the onion, ground beef, tomato, and jalapeños, and stir the ingredients. 2. Add in the seasoning mix, then add the chopped chipotles, and stir again. 3. Spray the inside of the pot with cooking spray. Add the meat-vegetable mixture to the pot and then stir in the milk and cheeses with a wooden spoon. 3. Cover the pot with lid. Turn dial to SLOW COOK, set temperature to LO, and set time to 2 hours. 4. When cooking is complete, stir the cheese dip again and serve.

Cheesy Jalapeño Poppers

Prep Time: 15 minutes | Cook Time: 4 hours | Serves: 12

8 ounces cream cheese, at room temperature
¼ cup sour cream
¼ cup grated Cheddar cheese

12 jalapeños, washed, seeded, and halved lengthwise
24 slices bacon
⅓ cup Chicken Stock or water

1. In a medium bowl, stir together the cream cheese, sour cream, and grated Cheddar cheese until well blended. 2. Divide the cheese mixture evenly among the jalapeño halves, and wrap each stuffed jalapeño half with a slice of bacon, and then secure the bacon with a toothpick. 3. In the pot, add the chicken stock and then add the stuffed jalapeños. 4. Cover the pot with lid. Turn dial to SLOW COOK, set temperature to LO, and set time to 4 hours. Cook on low for 4 hours or on high for 2 hours. 5. When cooking is complete, using a slotted spoon, remove the stuffed jalapeños from the pot and serve hot or at room temperature.

Sweet 'n' Spicy Snack Mix

Prep Time: 5 minutes | Cook Time: 1½ hours | Serves: 6

1 cup raw cashews
1 cup raw almonds
1 cup raw pecan halves
1 cup walnuts
½ cup raw pepitas
½ cup raw sunflower seeds

¼ cup aquafaba
¼ cup maple syrup
1 teaspoon miso paste
1 teaspoon garlic powder
1 teaspoon paprika
2 teaspoons ground ginger

1. Put the cashews, almonds, walnuts, pecans, pepitas, and sunflower seeds in the pot. 2. In a deep bowl, whisk or use an immersion blender to beat the aquafaba until foamy, about 1 minute. Add the maple syrup, garlic powder, miso paste, paprika, and ginger and whisk or blend to combine. Pour over the nuts in the pot and gently toss, making sure all the nuts and seeds are coated. 3. Stretch a clean dish towel or several layers of paper towels over the top of the pot, but not touching the food. 4. Cover the pot with lid. Turn dial to SLOW COOK, set temperature to LO, and set time to 1½ hours. Cook, stirring every 20 to 30 minutes to keep the nuts from burning. After each stir, dry any condensation under the lid and replace the towels before re-covering. 5. Line a rimmed baking sheet with parchment paper. When cooking is complete, transfer the snack mix to the baking sheet to cool. Store in an airtight container for up to 2 weeks.

Lemony Chickpea Snackers

Prep Time: 10 minutes | Cook Time: 8-10 hours | Serves: 7-8

4 (14.5-ounce) cans chickpeas, drained and rinsed
Juice of 2 lemons
1 tablespoon garlic powder

1 tablespoon onion powder
2 teaspoons paprika
Salt (optional)

1. Put the chickpeas into the pot. Add the lemon juice, onion powder, garlic powder, and paprika. Season with salt (if using). Toss gently to thoroughly coat every chickpea with the seasoning. 2. Cover the pot with lid. Turn dial to SLOW COOK, set temperature to LO, and set time to 8 hours. Cook on low for 8 to 10 hours or on high for 4 to 6 hours, stirring every 30 to 45 minutes to keep the chickpeas from burning. 3. Using a wooden spoon or a chopstick, prop open the lid to allow the steam to escape. 4. When cooking is complete, serve and enjoy.

Chile Cheese Dip

Prep Time: 20 minutes | Cook Time: 2 hours | Serves: 16

Cooking spray
1 medium onion, chopped
1 large tomato, seeded and chopped
3 medium jalapeños, seeded and chopped
1 medium poblano chile, seeded and chopped

1 garlic clove, minced
1 cup whole milk
8 ounces queso quesadilla or cream cheese, cut into 1-inch cubes
8 ounces grated American cheese, white or yellow

1. Spray the inside of the pot with cooking spray. 2. Add the onion, tomato, jalapeños, poblano chile, garlic, milk, and cheeses to the pot. Give everything a quick stir with a wooden spoon. 3. Cover the pot with lid. Turn dial to SLOW COOK, set temperature to LO, and set time to 2 hours. 4. When the cooking finishes, stir the dip and serve.

Parmesan Spaghetti Squash

Prep Time: 10 minutes | Cook Time: 8 hours | Serves: 6

1 spaghetti squash
¼ cup water
¼ cup olive oil

2 garlic cloves, minced
¼ cup low-fat grated Parmesan cheese

1. Prick the spaghetti squash all over with a fork. 2. Put the squash in the pot and add the water. 3. Cover with the lid. Turn dial to SLOW COOK, set temperature to LO, and set time to 8 hours. 4. When cooking is done, allow the squash to cool slightly. When it is cool enough to handle, cut the squash in half. 5. Scrape a fork across the squash flesh to make strands. 6. Turn dial to SEAR/SAUTÉ, set temperature to HI, and press START/STOP to begin preheating. Let the unit preheat for 5 minutes. 7. When preheating is complete, heat the olive oil in the pot. 8. Add the garlic and cook for 30 seconds. 9. Toss the spaghetti squash with the garlic and olive oil mixture and the Parmesan cheese.

Chapter 4 Poultry

Italian Chicken Thighs with Green Beans 49

Texas Barbecued Chicken Thighs 49

Wheat Berry Chicken Casserole 49

Lemony Garlic Chicken Thighs 50

Slow-cookedchicken Fajitas 50

Creamy Garlic Parmesan Chicken 50

Barbecue Pulled Chicken 51

Hearty White Bean,Chicken & Apple Cider

Chili 51

Buffalo Chicken Lettuce Wraps with Cherry

Tomatoes.. 51

Sweet Mustard Chicken Fillets 52

Spicy Rotisserie-Style Whole Chicken 52

Ground Turkey and Vegetables 52

Garlicky Turkey Breasts 53

Jerk Chicken Thighs 53

Turkey Meatballs in Tomato Sauce................ 53

Classic Jambalaya 54

Lemon-Garlic Chicken 54

Cheesy Turkey-Stuffed Peppers.................... 54

Southwest Chicken Breasts........................ 55

Savory Mandarin Orange Chicken 55

Slow-Cooked Sweet and Sour Chicken 55

Honey Teriyaki Chicken 56

Slow-Cooked Southwest Chicken 56

Garlic Turkey and Wild Rice 56

Delicious Cuban Chicken 57

Thai Panang Duck Curry 57

Flavorful Chicken Marsala 57

Thai Braised Chicken Thighs 58

Palatable Turkey and Gravy 58

Chili Cranberry Turkey Meatballs 58

Simple Cornish Hens in Plum Sauce 59

Slow-Cooked Crack Chicken 59

Authentic Caribbean Chicken Curry 59

Easy Teriyaki Chicken 60

Traditional Chicken Cordon Bleu 60

Ground Turkey Spaghetti Squash Casserole 60

Italian Chicken Thighs with Green Beans
Prep Time: 10 minutes | Cook Time: 9-10 hours | Serves: 4

2-pounds boneless, skinless chicken thighs
½ cup Italian salad dressing
3 russet potatoes, cut into wedges

3 cloves garlic, chopped
1 onion, chopped
1 (10-ounce) package frozen green beans, thawed

1. Combine chicken with salad dressing in a zipper-lock bag. Place in a large bowl or casserole and refrigerate for 6 to 7 hours. 2. When ready to cook, place potatoes, garlic, and onion in the pot. Pour chicken and salad dressing over all and cover with the lid. 3. Turn dial to SLOW COOK, set temperature to LO, and set time to 8 hours. 4. Then add green beans to pot and cover with the lid again. Continue to cook on low for 1 to 2 hours longer or until chicken is thoroughly cooked and vegetables are tender. 5. When cooking is complete, serve and enjoy.

Texas Barbecued Chicken Thighs
Prep Time: 10 minutes | Cook Time: 8-10 hours | Serves: 4

2 tablespoons vegetable oil
1 onion, chopped
2 cloves garlic, minced
1 jalapeño pepper, minced
¼ cup orange juice
1 tablespoon low-sodium soy sauce
2 tablespoons apple cider vinegar

2 tablespoons brown sugar
2 tablespoons Dijon mustard
1 (8-ounce) can tomato sauce
1 tablespoon chili powder
¼ teaspoon pepper
6 boneless, skinless, chicken thighs

1. Remove the lid from the pot. Turn dial to SEAR/SAUTÉ, set temperature to LO, and press START/STOP to begin preheating. Let the unit preheat for 5 minutes. 2. When preheating is complete, heat the oil in the pot. 3. Add the onion and garlic, cook, and stir until crisp and tender, about 4 minutes. Add jalapeño, soy sauce, vinegar, orange juice, brown sugar, mustard, tomato sauce, chili powder, and pepper. 4. Add chicken to the sauce, pushing chicken into the sauce to completely cover. Cover with the lid. Turn dial to SLOW COOK, set temperature to LO, and set time to 8 hours. Cook for 8 to 10 hours or until chicken is thoroughly cooked. 5. When cooking is complete, serve and enjoy.

Wheat Berry Chicken Casserole
Prep Time: 10 minutes | Cook Time: 8–9 hours 20–30 minutes | Serves: 6

1 cup wheat berries
1½ pounds boneless, skinless chicken thighs
3 carrots, sliced
2 cups frozen corn
1 onion, chopped
3 cloves garlic, minced

2 cups Chicken Stock
1 teaspoon cumin
1 teaspoon salt
¼ teaspoon pepper
1 tablespoon cornstarch
¼ cup water

1. Rinse the wheat berries and drain well. Cut the chicken into 1½-inch pieces and combine with the remaining ingredients, except for cornstarch and ¼ cup water, in the pot. Cover with the lid. Turn dial to SLOW COOK, set temperature to LO, and set time to 8 hours. Cook for 8 to 9 hours or until wheat berries are tender and chicken is cooked. 2. In a small bowl, combine the cornstarch and water and blend well. Add to casserole in the pot, cover again, and cook on high for 20 to 30 minutes until thickened. Then stir again and serve.

Lemony Garlic Chicken Thighs

Prep Time: 15 minutes | Cook Time: 7-8 hours | Serves: 4-6

2 cups chicken broth
1½ teaspoons garlic powder
1 teaspoon sea salt

Juice and zest of 1 large lemon
2 pounds boneless skinless chicken thighs

1. Pour the broth into the pot. 2. In a small bowl, stir together the salt, garlic powder, lemon juice, and lemon zest. Baste each chicken thigh with an even coating of the mixture. Place the thighs along the bottom of the pot and cover with the lid. 3. Turn dial to SLOW COOK, set temperature to LO, and set time to 7 hours. Cook for 7 to 8 hours until the internal temperature of the chicken reaches 165°F on a meat thermometer and the juices run clear, and serve.

Slow-cookedchicken Fajitas

Prep Time: 15 minutes | Cook Time: 7-8 hours | Serves: 4-6

1 (14.5-ounce) can diced tomatoes
1 (4-ounce) can Hatch green chiles
1½ teaspoons garlic powder
2 teaspoons chili powder
1½ teaspoons ground cumin
1 teaspoon paprika
1 teaspoon sea salt
Juice of 1 lime

Pinch cayenne pepper
Freshly ground black pepper
1 red bell pepper, seeded and sliced
1 green bell pepper, seeded and sliced
1 yellow bell pepper, seeded and sliced
1 large onion, sliced
2 pounds boneless, skinless chicken breast

1. In a medium bowl, mix up the diced tomatoes, chiles, garlic powder, cumin, paprika, chili powder, salt, lime juice, and cayenne, and season with black pepper. Mix well. Pour half the diced tomato mixture into the bottom of your pot. 2. Layer half the red, green, and yellow bell peppers and half the onion over the tomatoes in the pot. 3. Place the chicken on top of the peppers and onions. 4. Cover the chicken with the remaining red, green, and yellow bell peppers and onions. Pour the remaining tomato mixture on top. 5. Cover the pot with lid. Turn dial to SLOW COOK, set temperature to LO, and set time to 7 hours. Cook for 7 to 8 hours, or until the internal temperature of the chicken reaches 165°F on a meat thermometer and the juices run clear, and serve.

Creamy Garlic Parmesan Chicken

Prep Time: 15 minutes | Cook Time: 6 hours | Serves: 8

2 pounds boneless, skinless chicken thighs
½ cup (1 stick) unsalted butter, melted
12 ounces cremini or button mushrooms, halved or quartered
1 onion, diced
8 garlic cloves, minced
2 teaspoons paprika

2 teaspoons kosher salt
1 teaspoon freshly ground black pepper
1 cup chicken broth
8 ounces cream cheese
1 cup grated Parmesan cheese
Fresh parsley, for garnish

1. Put the chicken pieces in the pot. Pour the melted butter over the chicken. Add the mushrooms, onion, paprika, salt, garlic, and pepper and toss to coat the chicken pieces with the butter. 2. Cover the pot with lid. Turn dial to SLOW COOK, set temperature to LO, and set time to 6 hours. 3. When cooking is finished, transfer the chicken and vegetables to a serving platter. 4. Turn dial to SEAR/SAUTÉ, set temperature to LO, and press START/STOP to begin preheating. Let the unit preheat for 5 minutes. 6. When preheating is complete, combine the chicken broth, cream cheese, and Parmesan cheese in the pot. Cook, stirring, until the cream cheese is melted and fully combined, about 5 minutes. 7. Pour the sauce over the chicken, garnished with parsley, and serve.

Barbecue Pulled Chicken
Prep Time: 10 minutes | Cook Time: 8 hours | Serves: 6

4 bacon slices, diced
½ cup (1 stick) unsalted butter, melted
¼ cup red wine vinegar
¼ cup chicken broth
¼ cup tomato paste
¼ cup prepared mustard
1 tablespoon soy sauce or tamari

1 teaspoon fish sauce or additional soy sauce or tamari
¼ cup erythritol
2 teaspoons chili powder
1 teaspoon ground cumin
1 teaspoon cayenne pepper
1½ pounds boneless, skinless chicken thighs

1. Remove the lid from the pot. Turn dial to SEAR/SAUTÉ, set temperature to HI, and press START/STOP to begin preheating. Let the unit preheat for 5 minutes. 2. When preheating is complete, cook the bacon in the pot until browned and crisp, about 5 minutes. 3. Stir in the butter, red wine vinegar, tomato paste, mustard, soy sauce, fish sauce, erythritol, chili powder, chicken broth, cumin, and cayenne. 4. Add the chicken to the sauce and stir to coat. Cover the pot with lid. Turn dial to SLOW COOK, set temperature to LO, and set time to 8 hours. 5. Transfer the chicken to a bowl or work surface. Using two forks, shred the chicken and then put the shredded meat back to the sauce. Serve hot.

Hearty White Bean, Chicken & Apple Cider Chili

Prep Time: 15 minutes | Cook Time: 7-8 hours | Serves: 4-6

3 cups chopped cooked chicken
2 (15-ounce) cans white navy beans, rinsed well and drained
1 medium onion, chopped
1 (15-ounce) can diced tomatoes
3 cups Chicken Bone Broth or store-bought chicken broth
1 cup apple cider
2 bay leaves
1 tablespoon extra-virgin olive oil

2 teaspoons garlic powder
1 teaspoon chili powder
1 teaspoon sea salt
½ teaspoon ground cumin
¼ teaspoon ground cinnamon
Pinch cayenne pepper
Freshly ground black pepper
¼ cup apple cider vinegar

1. In the pot, combine the chicken, beans, broth, cider, bay leaves, onion, tomatoes, olive oil, garlic powder, chili powder, salt, cinnamon, cumin, and cayenne, and season with black pepper. 2. Cover the pot with lid. Turn dial to SLOW COOK, set temperature to LO, and set time to 7 hours. Cook for 7 to 8 hours. 3. Remove and discard the bay leaves. Stir in the apple cider vinegar until well blended and serve.

Buffalo Chicken Lettuce Wraps with Cherry Tomatoes

Prep Time: 15 minutes | Cook Time: 7-8 hours | Serves: 4-6

1 tablespoon extra-virgin olive oil
2 pounds boneless, skinless chicken breast
2 cups Vegan Buffalo Dip
1 cup water

8 to 10 romaine lettuce leaves
½ red onion, thinly sliced
1 cup cherry tomatoes, halved

1. Coat the bottom of the pot with the olive oil. 2. Add the chicken, dip, and water, and stir to combine. 3. Cover the pot with lid. Turn dial to SLOW COOK, set temperature to LO, and set time to 7 hours. Cook for 7 to 8 hours until the internal temperature of the chicken reaches 165°F on a meat thermometer and the juices run clear. 4. When cooking is complete, shred the chicken with a fork, and then mix it into the dip in the pot. 5. Divide the meat mixture among the lettuce leaves. Top with onion and tomato, and serve.

Sweet Mustard Chicken Fillets

Prep Time: 5 minutes | Cook Time: 6 hours | Serves: 6

6 chicken fillets, skinless, halved
¼ cup chicken broth
⅓ cup mustard, whole grain

¼ cup yacón syrup
Salt, pepper to taste

1. In a medium bowl, mix mustard together with syrup and chicken broth. 2. Place the fillets into the pot. 3. Pour the mustard mixture over the chicken, flavor with pepper and salt. 4. Cover the pot with lid. Turn dial to SLOW COOK, set temperature to LO, and set time to 6 hours. 5. When cooking is complete, serve and enjoy.

Spicy Rotisserie-Style Whole Chicken

Prep Time: 15 minutes | Cook Time: 8 hours | Serves: 8-10

1 tablespoon sea salt
1 teaspoon ground black pepper
2 teaspoons smoked paprika
½ teaspoon ground white pepper
½ teaspoon cayenne pepper

½ teaspoon garlic powder
½ teaspoon onion powder
½ teaspoon dried thyme
1 (5- to 6-pound) fresh whole chicken

1. To make the spice rub, in a small bowl, combine the salt, paprika, white pepper, black pepper, garlic powder, cayenne, onion powder, and thyme. 2. Remove the giblets from inside the chicken and use a paper towel to dry the interior. 3. Place 4 balls of aluminum foil in the bottom of the pot, this will be your chicken "rack". 4. Rub the outside and inside of the chicken with the spice rub, coating it well. 5. Place the chicken on the foil balls inside the pot and cover with the lid. Turn dial to SLOW COOK, set temperature to LO, and set time to 8 hours. Cook until the chicken is golden brown and cooked through or a meat thermometer inserted into the thigh or breast reads 165°F. 6. When cooking is complete, transfer the chicken to a rack or cutting board. Let rest for 5 minutes. 7. Slice the chicken and serve warm. 8. Refrigerate the leftovers for up to 1 week, or freeze for up to 2 months.

Ground Turkey and Vegetables

Prep Time: 15 minutes | Cook Time: 7-8 hours | Serves: 6-8

3 tablespoons extra-virgin olive oil
1 tablespoon minced garlic
1 large white onion, chopped
3 pounds ground turkey
1 large red bell pepper, cored and chopped
1 large yellow bell pepper, cored and chopped
1 large orange bell pepper, cored and chopped
1 large sweet potato, peeled and chopped
1 large zucchini, peeled and chopped

1 to 1½ cups water
2 teaspoons sea salt
½ teaspoon ground black pepper
3 tablespoons low-sodium soy sauce or coconut aminos
1 tablespoon dried oregano
2 teaspoons paprika
2 teaspoons chopped fresh parsley
½ lemon

1. Remove the lid from the pot. Turn dial to SEAR/SAUTÉ, set temperature to HI, and press START/STOP to begin preheating. Let the unit preheat for 5 minutes. 2. When preheating is complete, combine the olive oil, garlic, and onion in the pot. Cook on high, stirring occasionally, for 2 to 3 minutes, until fragrant. 3. Stir in the turkey, yellow bell pepper, red bell pepper, orange bell pepper, sweet potato, and zucchini. 4. Add the water, salt, oregano, paprika, black pepper, soy sauce, parsley, and a squeeze of lemon juice. Mix well and cover with the lid. 5. Turn dial to SLOW COOK, set temperature to LO, and set time to 7 hours. Cook for 7 to 8 hours until the turkey has cooked through and the vegetables are soft. 6. When cooking is complete, serve the turkey and vegetables warm. 7. Refrigerate leftovers for up to 1 week, or freeze for up to 2 months.

Garlicky Turkey Breasts
Prep Time: 15 minutes | Cook Time: 6 hours | Serves: 12

7 lb turkey breasts, no bones
4 cloves garlic, sliced
½ cup water

1 Tbsp yacón syrup
Salt, pepper to taste

1. Put all the ingredients into the pot. Make sure all turkey pieces are evenly coated. 2. Cover the pot with lid. Turn dial to SLOW COOK, set temperature to LO, and set time to 6 hours. 3. When cooking is complete, serve and enjoy.

Jerk Chicken Thighs
Prep Time: 20 minutes | Cook Time: 7-9 hours | Serves: 8

10 (4-ounce) boneless, skinless chicken thighs
2 tablespoons honey
3 tablespoons grated fresh ginger root
1 teaspoon ground red chili
1 tablespoon chili powder

½ teaspoon ground cloves
¼ teaspoon ground allspice
3 onions, chopped
6 garlic cloves, minced
½ cup freshly squeezed orange juice

1. Cut slashes across the chicken thighs so the flavorings can permeate. 2. In a small bowl, mix the honey, ground chili, ginger root, chili powder, cloves, and allspice. Rub this mixture into the chicken. Let the chicken stand while you prepare the vegetables. 3. In the bottom of pot, add the onions and garlic and top with the chicken. Pour the orange juice over all and cover the pot with lid. 4. Turn dial to SLOW COOK, set temperature to LO, and set time to 7 hours. Cook for 7 to 9 hours until a food thermometer registers 165°F. 5. When cooking is complete, serve.

Turkey Meatballs in Tomato Sauce
Prep Time: 15 minutes | Cook Time: 6-7 hours | Serves: 6-8

1 tablespoon extra-virgin olive oil
1 pound lean ground turkey
1 pound sweet Italian turkey sausage
¾ cup rolled oats
¼ cup fresh grated Parmesan cheese, plus more for topping (optional)
3 large eggs
¼ cup finely chopped fresh parsley, plus more for topping (optional)

¼ cup dried basil
½ teaspoon sea salt
½ teaspoon ground black pepper
2 teaspoons minced garlic
1 (28-ounce) jar no-sugar-added marinara sauce
1 (15-ounce) can crushed tomatoes
1 (15-ounce) can tomato sauce
1½ to 2 cups cooked whole-wheat pasta

1. Coat the bottom of pot with the olive oil. 2. In a large bowl, combine the ground turkey, turkey sausage, eggs, parsley, basil, salt, oats, cheese, black pepper, and garlic. Stir. 3. Form the turkey mixture into 1½-inch balls. Place the balls in a single layer on the bottom of the pot until the bottom is covered and you will probably have some meatballs left. 4. In a separate large bowl, mix together the marinara sauce, crushed tomatoes, and tomato sauce. 5. Pour one-third to half of the tomato mixture over top of the meatballs. 6. Repeat another layer of meatballs, and cover with the remaining sauce. Cover with the lid. 7. Turn dial to SLOW COOK, set temperature to LO, and set time to 6 hours. Cook for 6 to 7 hours until the meatballs have cooked through. 8. When cooking is complete, top with additional parsley and cheese if using. 9. Serve the meatballs warm over ¼ cup of pasta per serving. Refrigerate the leftovers for up to 1 week, or freeze for up to 3 months.

Classic Jambalaya

Prep Time: 20 minutes | Cook Time: 7½-9½ hours | Serves: 8

10 (4-ounce) boneless, skinless chicken thighs, cut into 2-inch pieces
2 onions, chopped
6 garlic cloves, minced
2 jalapeño peppers, minced
2 green bell peppers, stemmed, seeded, and chopped

5 celery stalks, sliced
2 cups Chicken Stock
1 tablespoon Cajun seasoning
¼ teaspoon cayenne pepper
1½ pounds raw shrimp, shelled and deveined

1. In the pot, mix the chicken, onions, garlic, celery, chicken stock, jalapeños, bell peppers, Cajun seasoning, and cayenne. Cover the pot with lid. 2. Turn dial to SLOW COOK, set temperature to LO, and set time to 7 hours. Cook for 7 to 9 hours until the chicken registers 165°F on a food thermometer. 3. Stir in the shrimp. Cover again and cook for another 30 to 40 minutes, or until the shrimp curl and turn pink. 4. When cooking is complete, serve and enjoy.

Lemon-Garlic Chicken

Prep Time: 10 minutes | Cook Time: 6 hours | Serves: 6

1 teaspoon dried oregano
¼ teaspoon freshly ground black pepper
2 pounds skinless, boneless chicken breast
1 tablespoon extra-virgin olive oil

¼ cup low-sodium chicken broth
3 tablespoons freshly squeezed lemon juice
2 teaspoons garlic, minced
¼ cup chopped fresh parsley

1. In a small bowl, mix together the oregano and black pepper. 2. Sprinkle the mixture evenly over the chicken. 3. Remove the lid from the pot. Turn dial to SEAR/SAUTÉ, set temperature to HI, and press START/STOP to begin preheating. Let the unit preheat for 5 minutes. 4. When preheating is complete, heat the olive oil in the pot. 5. Add the chicken and brown on both sides, about 3 minutes per side. 6. Add the broth, lemon juice, and garlic to the pot and bring the mixture to a gentle boil. 7. Cover the pot with lid. Turn dial to SLOW COOK, set temperature to LO, and set time to 6 hours. Cook on low for 6 hours or on high for 3 hours. 8. Sprinkle the parsley on top of the chicken about 15 to 30 minutes before the end of cooking time. 9. When cooking is complete, serve and enjoy. 10. Store leftover cooked chicken in the refrigerator in an airtight container for 3 to 4 days. Freeze it in airtight containers or heavy-duty freezer bags for up to 4 months.

Cheesy Turkery-Stuffed Peppers

Prep Time: 15 minutes | Cook Time: 7 hours 45 minutes | Serves: 6

1 pound lean ground turkey
1 tablespoon extra-virgin olive oil
2 teaspoons minced garlic
1 medium white onion, diced
1½ cups cooked rice
1½ teaspoons sea salt
¼ teaspoon ground black pepper
1 tablespoon dried basil

1 tablespoon dried parsley
6 yellow, orange, or red bell peppers, tops cut off and reserved, cored
¼ cup water
1 (24-ounce) jar marinara sauce
2 cups shredded mozzarella cheese
Grated Parmesan cheese, for topping
Fresh parsley, for topping

1. In a large bowl, combine the olive oil, turkey, rice, salt, garlic, onion, black pepper, basil, and dried parsley. Mix well. 2. Stuff each bell pepper evenly with the turkey mixture, then cover each bell pepper with its top. 3. Pour the water into the pot, then place each bell pepper inside, and cover the pot with lid. 4. Turn dial to SLOW COOK, set temperature to LO, and set time to 7 hours. Cook until the turkey has cooked through. 5. Remove the lid, pour the marinara sauce over the peppers, and sprinkle the mozzarella cheese evenly over the top of the sauce and bell peppers. Replace the lid and cook for an additional 30 to 45 minutes, until the cheese has melted. 6. When cooking is complete, top with Parmesan cheese and fresh parsley. Serve the peppers warm. 7. Refrigerate leftovers for up to 5 days, or freeze for up to 1 month.

Southwest Chicken Breasts

Prep Time: 15 minutes | Cook Time: 6 hours | Serves: 6

4 chicken breasts, with boneless, skinless, halved
1 zucchini, chopped
1 bell pepper, cubed

1 jar salsa, sugar free
Salt, pepper to taste

1. In a large bowl, stir the chicken breasts in salsa. 2. Put all the ingredients into the pot. Flavor with salt and pepper. 3. Cover the pot with lid. Turn dial to SLOW COOK, set temperature to LO, and set time to 6 hours. 4. When cooking is complete, serve and enjoy.

Savory Mandarin Orange Chicken

Prep Time: 10 minutes | Cook Time: 6 hours | Serves: 6

1½ pounds bone-in, skin-on chicken thighs
1 tablespoon Chinese five-spice powder
½ teaspoon kosher salt
6 bacon slices, diced
1 large orange, sliced
1 small red chile pepper, very thinly sliced, or ½ teaspoon
red pepper flakes
1 garlic clove, minced

1 tablespoon minced fresh ginger
¼ cup Asian sesame paste
2 tablespoons soy sauce or tamari
1 tablespoon freshly squeezed lime juice
1 tablespoon toasted sesame oil
1 tablespoon erythritol
¼ cup (½ stick) unsalted butter, cubed
½ cup chopped macadamia nuts

1. Season the chicken thighs all over with the five-spice powder and salt. Set aside. 2. Remove the lid from the pot. Turn dial to SEAR/SAUTÉ, set temperature to HI, and press START/STOP to begin preheating. Let the unit preheat for 5 minutes. 3. When preheating is complete, cook the bacon in the pot until crisp and browned, about 5 minutes. 4. Add the orange slices, red chile pepper, garlic, ginger, soy sauce, lime juice, sesame paste, sesame oil, and erythritol in the pot. Stir to mix and transfer the mixture to a large bowl. 5. In the pot on high heat, add the seasoned chicken, skin-side down. Sear until browned, about 3 minutes per side. 6. Arrange the browned chicken, skin-side up, and the mixture in the large bowl in the pot. Top with the butter pieces. 7. Cover the pot with lid. Turn dial to SLOW COOK, set temperature to LO, and set time to 6 hours. 8. When cooking is complete, serve hot, garnished with the macadamia nuts.

Slow-Cooked Sweet and Sour Chicken

Prep Time: 15 minutes | Cook Time: 4½ hours | Serves: 6

1 egg, beaten
½ cup all-purpose flour
1 pound chicken thighs or breasts, cut into bite-size pieces
1 tablespoon coconut oil (or oil of preference)
1 (6-ounce) can tomato paste
½ cup water
2 tablespoons apple cider vinegar

2 tablespoons brown sugar
2 tablespoons freshly grated ginger
1 small red onion, diced
1 bell pepper, diced
1 head broccoli, cut into florets
1½ cups fresh pineapple, diced

1. Put the egg and flour in separate, flat-bottomed bowls. 2. Dredge the chicken pieces into the egg, and dredge in the flour. 3. Remove the lid from the pot. Turn dial to SEAR/SAUTÉ, set temperature to HI, and press START/STOP to begin preheating. Let the unit preheat for 5 minutes. 4. When preheating is complete, heat the oil in the pot. Add the chicken and brown, about 20 to 30 seconds per side. Set aside. 5. Add the tomato paste, water, sugar, vinegar, and ginger to the pot and mix to combine. 6. Add the onion, broccoli, bell pepper, and pineapple and stir. Top with the chicken and stir until all ingredients are coated with sauce. 7. Cover the pot with lid. Turn dial to SLOW COOK, set temperature to LO, and set time to 4½ hours. Cook on low for 4½ hours or on high for 2½ hours. 8. When cooking is complete, serve and enjoy.

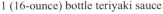

Honey Teriyaki Chicken

Prep Time: 10 minutes | Cook Time: 6-8 hours | Serves: 6-8

1 (16-ounce) bottle teriyaki sauce
¼ cup honey
4 garlic cloves, minced
Pinch red pepper flakes

2½ pounds bone-in skinless chicken thighs
Steamed white rice, for serving
4 scallions, thinly sliced, for serving
2 tablespoons sesame seeds, for serving

1. In the pot, whisk together the teriyaki sauce, garlic, honey, and red pepper flakes. Add the chicken to the pot and turn the pieces to coat them in the sauce. 2. Cover the pot with lid. Turn dial to SLOW COOK, set temperature to LO, and set time to 6 hours. Cook for 6 to 8 hours until the chicken is tender. 3. When cooking is complete, spoon over steamed rice and garnish with the scallions and sesame seeds.

Slow-Cooked Southwest Chicken

Prep Time: 10 minutes | Cook Time: 8-10 hours | Serves: 6

2 teaspoons chili powder
1 teaspoon cumin
1 teaspoon paprika
¼ teaspoon oregano
¼ to ½ teaspoon cayenne pepper (optional)
1 pound boneless, skinless chicken breasts
1 green bell pepper, chopped

1 medium onion, diced
2 garlic cloves, minced
½ teaspoon freshly ground black pepper
1 (14.5-ounce) can no-salt-added, diced tomatoes, undrained
1 (3-ounce) can green chilies
1 cup low-sodium chicken broth

1. In a small bowl, stir together chili powder, paprika, cumin, oregano, and cayenne (if using). 2. Place the chicken into the pot and sprinkle half of the seasoning mixture over. Flip the chicken with a fork and sprinkle with the remaining half of seasoning mixture. 3. Place the bell pepper, onion, garlic, tomatoes, black pepper, and chilies over the chicken and pour the chicken broth on top. 4. Cover the pot with lid. Turn dial to SLOW COOK, set temperature to LO, and set time to 8 hours. Cook on low for 8 to 10 hours or on high for 3 to 4 hours. The chicken will break apart easily with a fork once cooked. 5. Store leftover cooked chicken in the refrigerator in an airtight container for 3 to 4 days. Freeze it in airtight containers or heavy-duty freezer bags for up to 4 months.

Garlic Turkey and Wild Rice

Prep Time: 10 minutes | Cook Time: 20-25 minutes | Serves: 6

3 cups water
1½ cups wild rice
1 tablespoon extra-virgin olive oil
1 cup chopped green bell pepper
2 celery stalks, cut into 1-inch pieces

2 medium carrots cut into 1-inch pieces
1 yellow onion, finely chopped
4 garlic cloves, minced
1 pound boneless turkey breast, cut into 1-inch cubes
1 (14.5-ounce) can no-salt stewed tomatoes

1. In a saucepan, bring the water to a boil. Add the rice and stir. Reduce the heat, cover, and simmer for 20 to 25 minutes. 2. When cooking the rice, make the turkey. Remove the lid from the pot. Turn dial to SEAR/SAUTÉ, set temperature to HI, and press START/STOP to begin preheating. Let the unit preheat for 5 minutes. 3. When preheating is complete, heat the olive oil in the pot. Add the bell pepper, celery, onion, carrots, and garlic and sauté until tender, 2 to 3 minutes. 4. Add the turkey and continue to sauté for 2 to 3 minutes. Turn the pieces over and continue cooking until the turkey loses its outer pink color, 2 to 3 minutes more. 5. Stir in the tomatoes and cover. Continue to simmer, stirring occasionally, until the turkey is cooked through and an instant-read thermometer registers 160°F. 6. When cooking is complete, serve over the hot wild rice. 7. Store leftover turkey in the refrigerator in an airtight container for 3 to 4 days. Freeze it in airtight containers or heavy-duty freezer bags for 2 to 3 months.

Delicious Cuban Chicken
Prep Time: 10 minutes | Cook Time: 6-8 hours | Serves: 6-8

½ cup minced fresh parsley
2 teaspoons dried oregano
Zest and juice of 1 lime
Zest and juice of 1 orange
½ cup pepper-stuffed olives
¼ cup raisins
2 green bell peppers, sliced
1 medium onion, halved and thinly sliced

8 garlic cloves, peeled and smashed
2 pounds bone-in skinless chicken thighs
1 pound Yukon Gold potatoes, cut into 2-inch pieces
2 cups Low-Sodium Chicken Broth, or store-bought
Sea salt
Freshly ground black pepper
1 cup frozen peas, thawed

1. Combine the parsley, oregano, lime zest and juice, olives, raisins, bell peppers, onion, garlic, orange zest and juice, chicken, potatoes, and chicken broth in the pot. Stir gently to mix. Season generously with black pepper and salt. 2. Cover the pot with lid. Turn dial to SLOW COOK, set temperature to LO, and set time to 6 hours. Cook for 6 to 8 hours until the chicken is cooked through and the potatoes are tender. 3. When cooking is complete, stir in the peas before serving.

Thai Panang Duck Curry
Prep Time: 10 minutes | Cook Time: 6-8 hours | Serves: 6-8

¼ cup panang curry paste
1 (14-ounce) can coconut milk
¼ cup brown sugar
Juice of 1 lime
2½ pounds bone-in skinless duck legs

8 ounces green beans, trimmed and cut into 2-inch pieces
1 (18-ounce) can pineapple chunks, drained
2 green bell peppers, sliced
1 cup roughly chopped fresh basil

1. Whisk together the curry paste, brown sugar, coconut milk, and lime juice in the pot. 2. Add the duck, pineapple, green beans, and bell peppers to the pot. 3. Cover the pot with lid. Turn dial to SLOW COOK, set temperature to LO, and set time to 6 hours. Cook for 6 to 8 hours. 4. Stir in the basil after cooking. Serve and enjoy.

Flavorful Chicken Marsala
Prep Time: 10 minutes | Cook Time: 6-8 hours | Serves: 6-8

½ cup marsala wine
1 cup Low-Sodium Chicken Broth, or store-bought
2 pounds boneless skinless chicken thighs
2 cups sliced mushrooms
1 small red onion or 4 shallots, minced
4 garlic cloves, minced

2 teaspoons fresh thyme
Sea salt
Freshly ground black pepper
2 tablespoons butter, melted
2 tablespoons all-purpose flour

1. Combine the wine, chicken broth, chicken, onion, garlic, mushrooms, and thyme in the pot. Stir gently to mix. Season with black pepper and salt. 2. Cover the pot with lid. Turn dial to SLOW COOK, set temperature to LO, and set time to 6 hours. Cook for 6 to 8 hours until the chicken is cooked through. 3. Using a slotted spoon, transfer the chicken and mushrooms to a serving plate. 4. Turn dial to SEAR/SAUTÉ, set temperature to HI, and simmer, uncovered, for another 15 minutes, until the sauce is reduced by about a third. 5. In a small bowl, stir the melted butter and flour together and then whisk it into the sauce in the pot. Simmer until the sauce is thickened, about 2 minutes. 6. When cooking is complete, pour the sauce over the chicken and mushrooms and serve.

Thai Braised Chicken Thighs

Prep Time: 10 minutes | Cook Time: 2½ hours | Serves: 4

4 boneless, skinless chicken thighs
3 tablespoons soy sauce
3 tablespoons chicken or vegetable broth
3 tablespoons lime juice

1 knob ginger, minced (or 1 teaspoon ground ginger)
1 shallot, thinly sliced
2 cloves garlic, thinly sliced
¼ teaspoon white pepper

1. Place all ingredients into the pot. 2. Cover the pot with lid. Turn dial to SLOW COOK, set temperature to HI, and set time to 2½ hours. 3. When cooking is complete, discard the cooking liquid before serving.

Palatable Turkey and Gravy

Prep Time: 10 minutes | Cook Time: 8 hours | Serves: 8

1¾ cups turkey or chicken broth
2 stalks celery
1 large carrot
1 medium onion, peeled and quartered
1 (3-pound) boneless turkey breast

1 teaspoon Mrs. Dash Seasoning Blend
2 tablespoons Madeira wine (optional)
¼ cup (Wondra) instant flour
Salt and freshly ground black pepper, to taste

1. Add the broth to the pot. 2. Cut each celery stalk in half. Scrub and cut the carrot into four pieces. Add the carrot, celery, and onion to the pot. 3. Nestle the turkey breast on top of the vegetables and sprinkle the seasoning blend over it. 4. Cover the pot with lid. Turn dial to SLOW COOK, set temperature to LO, and set time to 8 hours. 5. Remove the turkey breast to a serving platter, cover and keep warm. 6. Strain the pot juices through a cheesecloth-lined colander set over a large nonstick skillet, squeezing the vegetables in the cheesecloth to release the juices. 7. Transfer ¼ cup of the broth to a bowl and mix it together with the Madeira and instant flour; stir until the flour is dissolved. Bring the broth to a boil over medium-high heat. 8. Whisk the flour mixture into the broth, stirring constantly until the gravy is thickened and coats the back of a spoon. Taste for seasoning, and add salt and pepper if needed. 9. Slice the turkey and pour the gravy over the top of the slices, or serve the gravy on the side.

Chili Cranberry Turkey Meatballs

Prep Time: 10 minutes | Cook Time: 4 hours | Serves: 12

28 ounces frozen, precooked turkey meatballs (about 24 meatballs)
¼ cup chili sauce

2 (14–16 ounce) cans whole-berry cranberry sauce
1½ packed tablespoons dark brown sugar
1 tablespoon ginger preserves

1. Defrost the meatballs according to package instructions. Mix together the chili sauce, brown sugar, cranberry sauce, and preserves in a large bowl. 2. Pour half of the sauce into the bottom of pot. Place the meatballs on top. Pour the remaining sauce over the meatballs. 3. Cover the pot with lid. Turn dial to SLOW COOK, set temperature to LO, and set time to 4 hours. Cook on low for 4 hours or on high for 2 hours. 4. When cooking is complete, serve and enjoy.

Simple Cornish Hens in Plum Sauce

Prep Time: 10 minutes | Cook Time: 6-8 hours | Serves: 4

Nonstick spray
1 cup Plum Sauce
2 tablespoons soy sauce
1 teaspoon ground ginger

1 teaspoon Chinese five-spice powder
2 Cornish hens
2 green onions, green parts thinly sliced (for garnish)
Toasted sesame seeds (for garnish)

1. Spray the inside of pot with nonstick spray. 2. In a medium bowl, mix the plum sauce, soy sauce, ginger, and five-spice powder. 3. Place hens in the prepared pot, breast side down. Brush with half the plum sauce mixture. 4. Cover the pot with lid. Turn dial to SLOW COOK, set temperature to LO, and set time to 4 hours. 5. Brush with remaining sauce. Re-cover and continue to cook for another 2 to 4 hours, or until juices run clear when pierced with a knife. Serve the hens garnished with green onions and/or sesame seeds, if desired.

Slow-Cooked Crack Chicken

Prep Time: 10 minutes | Cook Time: 4-6 hours | Serves: 8

2 pounds boneless, skinless chicken breasts
½ cup water
8 ounces low-fat cream cheese

2 tablespoons Homemade Ranch Seasoning
6 slices bacon, cooked and chopped
1 cup shredded low-fat Cheddar cheese

1. Add the chicken, water, and cream cheese to the pot. Sprinkle the ranch seasoning on top. Stir to mix well. 2. Cover the pot with lid. Turn dial to SLOW COOK, set temperature to LO, and set time to 4 hours. Cook on low for 4 to 6 hours or on high for 2 to 3 hours. 3. Remove the chicken and shred it using two forks. 4. Add the chicken back into the pot along with the bacon. Stir to mix well. Top with the Cheddar cheese and serve.

Authentic Caribbean Chicken Curry

Prep Time: 15 minutes | Cook Time: 6-8 hours | Serves: 6

3 pounds boneless, skin-on chicken thighs or other dark meat
1 onion, chopped
2 garlic cloves, minced
1 jalapeño pepper, chopped
½ cup coconut milk

1 tablespoon curry powder
1 teaspoon allspice
½ teaspoon cloves
½ teaspoon nutmeg
1 teaspoon ground ginger

1. Add the chicken, onion, garlic, jalapeño, curry powder, allspice, cloves, nutmeg, coconut milk, and ginger to the pot. Stir to mix well. 2. Cover the pot with lid. Turn dial to SLOW COOK, set temperature to LO, and set time to 6 hours. Cook on low for 6 to 8 hours or on high for 3 to 4 hours. 3. When cooking is complete, serve and enjoy.

Easy Teriyaki Chicken

Prep Time: 5 minutes | Cook Time: 1 hour | Serves: 6

1 pound frozen chicken nuggets, defrosted
5–6 ounces teriyaki sauce

1 teaspoon hot sauce

1. In the pot, combine all ingredients. 2. Cover the pot with lid. Turn dial to SLOW COOK, set temperature to LO, and set time to 1 hour. 3. When cooking is complete, serve hot.

Traditional Chicken Cordon Bleu

Prep Time: 10 minutes | Cook Time: 4-6 hours | Serves: 6

Cooking spray
2 pounds boneless, skinless chicken breasts
8 ounces uncured ham, sliced

8 ounces Swiss cheese, sliced
1¾ cups Cream of Mushroom Sauce
1 tablespoon unsalted butter, cut into small pieces

1. Coat the pot generously with cooking spray. 2. Place the chicken in the bottom of the pot. Place the ham slices over the chicken. Place the cheese on top. 3. Pour the mushroom sauce over the top and spread it evenly with a spoon. 4. Scatter pieces of butter over the top. 5. Cover the pot with lid. Turn dial to SLOW COOK, set temperature to LO, and set time to 4 hours. Cook on low for 4 to 6 hours or on high for 2 to 3 hours. 6. When cooking is complete, serve and enjoy.

Ground Turkey Spaghetti Squash Casserole

Prep Time: 10 minutes | Cook Time: 6-8 hours | Serves: 8

2 pounds 93% lean ground turkey
1 (28-ounce) can low-sodium or no-salt-added diced tomatoes
¼ cup Parmesan cheese
1 cup shredded part-skim mozzarella cheese
1 small onion, diced

2 garlic cloves, minced
2 tablespoons Italian seasoning
½ teaspoon salt
1 (2-pound) spaghetti squash
Chopped fresh herbs, such as rosemary or thyme, for garnish (optional)

1. Add the turkey, tomatoes, Parmesan, onion, garlic, Italian seasoning, mozzarella, and salt to the pot. Stir to mix well. 2. Halve the spaghetti squash crosswise and scoop out and discard the seeds. Place the halves cut-side down in the pot. 3. Cover the pot with lid. Turn dial to SLOW COOK, set temperature to LO, and set time to 6 hours. Cook on low for 6 to 8 hours or on high for 3 to 4 hours. 4. Remove the spaghetti squash from the pot, using oven mitts to protect your hands. Let the squash cool for about 5 minutes, then rake a fork across the flesh to remove it in spaghetti-like strands. 5. Add the spaghetti squash strands back into the pot and mix until well combined. Garnish with fresh herbs, if using, and serve.

Chapter 5 Beef, Pork, and Lambs

Mustard Pork and Beans 62

Bay Beef Bone Broth 62

Chili Pork Tenderloin 62

Beef and Bell Peppers Stew 63

Korean-Style Beef Lettuce Wraps 63

Savory Maple-Balsamic Lamb Shoulder 63

Herbed Pork Loin with Dried Fruit................ 64

Curried Pork Chops with Bell Peppers 64

Classic Steak Diane.................................. 64

Roast Pork with Cabbage and Pears 65

Pork Roast with Honey-Mustard Sauce 65

Tender Pork with Potatoes and Sweet Potatoes ... 65

Delicious Beef Enchilada Casserole 66

Beef Stew with Vegetables 66

Tasty Braised Beef and Pork with Green Salsa ... 66

Yucatec-Style Roasted Pork 67

Cheese Meatballs in Tomato Sauce 67

Italian Stuffed Meatloaf 68

Slow-Cooked Shredded Beef 68

Pork Chops with Sweet Potatoes 68

Classic Beef Meatloaf............................... 69

Sunday Pot Roast with Gravy....................... 69

Tender Shredded Beef Ragu 69

Pork Tenderloin with Peach Sauce 70

Mediterranean Beef with Pearl Barley 70

Traditional Beef Cholent............................ 70

Hearty Red Wine Beef Stew 71

Tender Flanken Ribs in Spicy Tomato Sauce 71

Slow-Cooked Jerk Pork Chops 71

Homemade Sephardic Cholent 72

Lamb in Coconut Curry Sauce 72

Mustard Pork and Beans

Prep Time: 10 minutes | Cook Time: 8-9 hours | Serves: 4

¾ pound boneless pork loin, cubed
½ teaspoon salt
½ teaspoon paprika
⅛ teaspoon pepper
1 (16-ounce) can pork and beans

1 onion, chopped
¼ cup ketchup
3 tablespoons mustard
2 tablespoons honey

1. Sprinkle pork with salt, paprika, and pepper, and rub into meat. Open pork and beans and drain off half of the thick liquid. Pour half of the can of pork and beans into the pot and add onions, mustard, ketchup, and honey; mix well. 2. Place half of the pork in the pot and top with remaining slightly drained pork and beans, then top with remaining pork. Cover the pot with lid. 3. Turn dial to SLOW COOK, set temperature to LO, and set time to 8 hours. Cook for 8 to 9 hours until meat is thoroughly cooked and tender. 4. When cooking is complete, serve and enjoy.

Bay Beef Bone Broth

Prep Time: 15 minutes | Cook Time: 18-24 hours | Serves: 10

2 pounds beef marrow bones
2 cups roughly chopped onions, celery, carrots, garlic, or scraps (a combination based on what's on hand or what you've saved)

2 bay leaves
1 tablespoon apple cider vinegar
Filtered water, to cover the ingredients

1. In your pot, combine the bones, onion, garlic, bay leaves, celery, carrots, and vinegar. Add enough water to cover the ingredients. 2. Cover the pot with lid. Turn dial to SLOW COOK, set temperature to LO, and set time to 18 hours. Cook for 18 to 24 hours. The longer it cooks, the more nutrients you get from the bones and vegetables. 3. Skim off and discard any foam from the surface. Ladle the broth through a fine-mesh sieve or cheesecloth into a large bowl. Transfer to airtight containers to store. 4. Keep refrigerated for 3 to 4 days. Freeze any excess for up to 3 months.

Chili Pork Tenderloin

Prep Time: 10 minutes | Cook Time: 6 hours | Serves: 8

2 tablespoons extra-virgin olive oil
1 medium yellow onion, diced
1 teaspoon garlic powder
1 teaspoon onion powder
1 teaspoon sea salt
1 teaspoon ground black pepper

¼ cup coconut sugar
1 tablespoon chili powder
1 tablespoon smoked paprika
4 pounds boneless pork loin
2 cups Savory Chicken Broth or store-bought chicken broth

1. Remove the lid from the pot. Turn dial to SEAR/SAUTÉ, set temperature to HI, and press START/STOP to begin preheating. Let the unit preheat for 5 minutes. 2. When preheating is complete, combine the olive oil and onion in the pot. Cook for 2 to 3 minutes, stirring occasionally, until the onion begins to sizzle. 3. In a small bowl, mix together the salt, garlic powder, onion powder, black pepper, sugar, chili powder, and paprika. 4. Thoroughly season the pork with the spice mixture. Add to the pot. 5. Add the broth and cover the pot with lid. 6. Turn dial to SLOW COOK, set temperature to LO, and set time to 6 hours. Cook for 6 hours until the pork has cooked through. 7. Turn off the pot. Spoon the broth from the bottom of the pot over the meat, and serve warm. 8. Refrigerate the leftovers for up to 1 week, or freeze for up to 3 months.

Beef and Bell Peppers Stew

Prep Time: 15 minutes | Cook Time: 6-7 hours | Serves: 4-6

1 pound beef tenderloin, cut into 1-inch chunks
1 red bell pepper, seeded and roughly chopped
1 yellow bell pepper, seeded and roughly chopped
1 green bell pepper, seeded and roughly chopped
1 medium onion, chopped
1 (14-ounce) can diced tomatoes
1 cup Beef Bone Broth or store-bought broth of choice

¼ cup coconut aminos
1½ teaspoons garlic powder
1 teaspoon coconut sugar
½ teaspoon ground ginger
Dash hot sauce (optional)
Freshly ground black pepper

1. In your pot, combine the beef, all bell peppers, onion, tomatoes, broth, coconut aminos, garlic powder, coconut sugar, ginger, and hot sauce if using, and season with black pepper. 2. Cover the pot with lid. Turn dial to SLOW COOK, set temperature to LO, and set time to 6 hours. Cook for 6 to 7 hours. 3. When cooking is complete, serve and enjoy.

Korean-Style Beef Lettuce Wraps

Prep Time: 15 minutes | Cook Time: 7-8 hours | Serves: 4-6

2 pounds beef chuck roast
1 small white onion, diced
1 cup broth of choice
3 tablespoons coconut aminos
2 tablespoons coconut sugar
1 tablespoon rice vinegar
1 teaspoon garlic powder

1 teaspoon sesame oil
½ teaspoon ground ginger
¼ teaspoon red pepper flakes
8 romaine lettuce leaves
1 tablespoon sesame seeds (optional)
2 scallions (both white and green parts), diced (optional)

1. In your pot, combine the beef, onion, broth, sesame oil, coconut sugar, vinegar, coconut aminos, garlic powder, ginger, and red pepper flakes. 2. Cover the pot with lid. Turn dial to SLOW COOK, set temperature to LO, and set time to 7 hours. Cook for 7 to 8 hours. 3. When cooking is complete, scoop spoonfuls of the beef mixture into each lettuce leaf. Garnish with the sesame seeds and diced scallion if using and serve.

Savory Maple-Balsamic Lamb Shoulder

Prep Time: 15 minutes | Cook Time: 8-10 hours | Serves: 6-8

2 tablespoons extra-virgin olive oil
3 to 4 pounds lamb shoulder, trimmed of excess fat
1 cup beef broth or chicken broth
1 cup aged balsamic vinegar
1 tablespoon onion powder
⅔ cup pure maple syrup
1 teaspoon minced garlic

1 tablespoon dried oregano
2 teaspoons dried sage
1 teaspoon sea salt
1 teaspoon ground black pepper
2 tablespoons feta cheese, for topping
Arugula, for topping

1. Coat the bottom of pot with the olive oil. 2. Place the lamb in the pot, with the fattiest part on top. 3. Add the broth, vinegar, maple syrup, onion powder, garlic, oregano, salt, sage, and black pepper on top of the lamb, letting the liquid fall over the sides of the lamb. Cover the pot with lid. 4. Turn dial to SLOW COOK, set temperature to LO, and set time to 7 hours. Cook for 7 to 8 hours until the lamb is tender and cooked through. 5. Remove the lid and transfer the lamb to a cutting board or platter. Cut it into 1- to 2-inch chunks, or shred it using 2 forks. Return it to the pot and stir. Replace the lid and cook for another 5 to 10 minutes. 6. Turn off the pot. Top with the cheese and arugula. Serve the lamb warm. 7. Refrigerate leftovers for up to 1 week, or freeze for up to 2 months.

Herbed Pork Loin with Dried Fruit

Prep Time: 20 minutes | Cook Time: 7-9 hours | Serves: 8

2 leeks, sliced
1 cup dried apricots
1 cup dried pears, sliced
½ cup golden raisins

1 (3-pound) boneless pork loin
½ teaspoon salt
1 teaspoon dried thyme leaves
1 cup apricot nectar

1. In the pot, place the leeks, apricots, pears, and raisins. Top with the pork. Sprinkle the pork with the salt and thyme. 2. Pour the apricot nectar around the pork, over the fruit. 3. Cover the pot with lid. Turn dial to SLOW COOK, set temperature to LO, and set time to 7 hours. Cook for 7 to 9 hours until the pork registers at least 150°F on a food thermometer. 4. When cooking is complete, serve and enjoy.

Curried Pork Chops with Bell Peppers

Prep Time: 20 minutes | Cook Time: 7-8 hours | Serves: 8

2 onions, chopped
4 garlic cloves, minced
2 red bell peppers, stemmed, seeded, and chopped
2 yellow bell peppers, stemmed, seeded, and chopped
8 (5.5-ounce) bone-in pork loin chops

½ teaspoon salt
1 tablespoon curry powder
1 tablespoon grated fresh ginger root
1 cup Chicken Stock

1. In the pot, mix the onions, garlic, and bell peppers. Add the pork chops to the pot, nestling them into the vegetables. 2. In a small bowl, mix the salt, ginger root, curry powder, and chicken stock, and pour into the pot 3. Cover the pot with lid. Turn dial to SLOW COOK, set temperature to LO, and set time to 7 hours. Cook for 7 to 8 hours until the pork chops are very tender. 4. When cooking is complete, serve and enjoy.

Classic Steak Diane

Prep Time: 20 minutes | Cook Time: 8-10 hours | Serves: 8

2 onions, sliced
4 garlic cloves, sliced
2 shallots, peeled and sliced
2 cups sliced cremini mushrooms
5 large carrots, sliced
1 (3-pound) grass-fed chuck shoulder roast or tri-tip roast,

cut into 2-inch pieces
2 tablespoons chopped fresh chives
1 teaspoon dried marjoram leaves
1 cup low-sodium beef broth
2 tablespoons butter

1. In the pot, mix the onions, shallots, garlic, mushrooms, and carrots. 2. Add the beef and stir gently. Sprinkle the chives and marjoram over the beef, and pour the beef broth over all. 3. Cover the pot with lid. Turn dial to SLOW COOK, set temperature to LO, and set time to 8 hours. Cook for 8 to 10 hours until the beef is very tender. 4. When cooking is complete, stir in the butter and serve.

Roast Pork with Cabbage and Pears

Prep Time: 20 minutes | Cook Time: 7-9 hours | Serves: 8

1 large head red cabbage, chopped
2 red onions, chopped
2 medium pears, peeled and chopped
4 garlic cloves, minced
1 cup Chicken Stock

¼ cup apple cider vinegar
3 tablespoons honey
1 teaspoon dried thyme leaves
½ teaspoon salt
1 (3-pound) pork loin roast

1. In the pot, mix the cabbage, pears, onions, and garlic. 2. In a small bowl, mix the vinegar, thyme, honey, salt, and chicken stock, and pour into the pot. 3. Top with the pork, nestling the meat into the vegetables. 4. Cover the pot with lid. Turn dial to SLOW COOK, set temperature to LO, and set time to 7 hours. Cook for 7 to 9 hours until the pork is tender. 5. When cooking is complete, serve and enjoy.

Pork Roast with Honey-Mustard Sauce

Prep Time: 10 minutes | Cook Time: 7-8 hours | Serves: 8

1 onion, chopped
4 cloves garlic, minced
⅓ cup honey mustard
1 tsp salt
¼ tsp pepper

1 tsp dried thyme
3-lb pork roast
¼ cup chicken broth
1 Tbsp cornstarch
¼ cup water

1. Coat the pot with nonstick cooking spray and add onions and garlic. 2. Rub salt and pepper and honey mustard over the pork roast. Sprinkle with thyme. 3. Place coated roast on top of onions and garlic. Pour the chicken broth. Cover the pot with lid. Turn dial to SLOW COOK, set temperature to LO, and set time to 7 hours. Cook for 7 to 8 hours. 4. Remove roast and cover with foil while making the sauce. 5. Combine the cornstarch and water in a medium saucepan and blend with a wire whisk. 6. Add juices from the pot and the cooked onions and garlic to the saucepan. Cook over medium heat, stirring. Remove the heat when the mixture thickens. 7. Season to taste. Add more salt, pepper, thyme, or honey mustard if needed. A pot mutes these flavors because of its long cooking time. 8. Slice the roast and serve it with the sauce.

Tender Pork with Potatoes and Sweet Potatoes

Prep Time: 15 minutes | Cook Time: 8-9 hours | Serves: 6

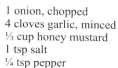

1 lb small red potatoes, cut in half
1 lb sweet potatoes, peeled and cut into chunks
2 red bell peppers, cut into large pieces
1 (3-lb) boneless pork loin roast
¼ cup Dijon mustard

1 tsp dried thyme
½ tsp salt
⅛ tsp black pepper
1½ cups low sodium beef broth

1. Place potatoes and bell peppers in the bottom of pot. 2. In a small bowl, mix mustard, salt, thyme, and black pepper and spread evenly over the pork. 3. Lay the pork out on top of the vegetables in the pot and pour the beef broth over all. 4. Cover the pot with lid. Turn dial to SLOW COOK, set temperature to LO, and set time to 8 hours. Cook for 8 to 9 hours. 5. When cooking is complete, slice the pork and serve with the vegetables and juices.

Delicious Beef Enchilada Casserole

Prep Time: 10 minutes | Cook Time: 4 hours | Serves: 4-6

1½ pounds lean ground beef
1 cup chopped onion
1 can (10¾ oz) condensed cream of mushroom soup
1 can (10¾ oz) condensed cream of chicken soup
1 can (4 oz) diced green chilies
1 Tbsp chili powder
½ tsp ground cumin

1 can (15 oz) pinto beans, drained
⅓ cup water
1½ to 2 cups shredded Cheddar or Jack cheese, or combination
10 to 12 corn tortillas
Salsa, sour cream, sliced green onions, cilantro, or guacamole, for garnish.

1. In a large skillet over medium heat, cook the ground beef and the chopped onions, stirring, until the beef is no longer pink. 2. Drain the ground beef and discard excess grease. To the ground beef, add the two condensed soups, the diced green chile peppers, chili powder, cumin, drained pinto beans, and water. Mix to blend thoroughly. 3. Spoon some of the ground beef and bean mixture into the bottom of a pot. 4. Layer with some tortillas and then add more ground beef mixture, shredded cheese, and tortillas. Repeat layers until all of the ingredients are used. Amounts and the number of layers might vary depending on the size or dimensions of your pot. 5. Cover the pot with lid. Turn dial to SLOW COOK, set temperature to LO, and set time to 4 hours. 6. When cooking is complete, serve and enjoy.

Beef Stew with Vegetables

Prep Time: 15 minutes | Cook Time: 10 hours | Serves: 6

3 pounds lean, boneless beef roast
4 cups Beef Stock
4 celery ribs, chopped
3 poblano chiles, diced
2 red bell peppers, diced
2 carrots, chopped
1 onion, chopped
1 habanero chile, left whole

1 bay leaf
4 garlic cloves, crushed
2 large tomatoes, diced
1 teaspoon dried Mexican oregano
1 teaspoon ground cumin
1 teaspoon sea salt
½ cup sliced Spanish olives

1. Spray the pot with cooking spray. 2. In the pot, combine all the ingredients, except the olives. 3. Cover the pot with lid. Turn dial to SLOW COOK, set temperature to LO, and set time to 10 hours. 4. Remove the habanero. 5. Transfer the beef to a cutting board and shred it using two forks. Return the shredded beef to the pot and stir it into the broth. 6. Serve with rice topped with the olives.

Tasty Braised Beef and Pork with Green Salsa

Prep Time: 5 minutes | Cook Time: 18 hours | Serves: 6

Cooking spray
1½ pounds lean, boneless beef roast
1½ pounds lean, boneless pork roast
2 tablespoons Fajita Seasoning Mix

1 cup Green Salsaor 1 (14.5-ounce) can green enchilada sauce
2 poblano chiles, fire-roasted, peeled, seeded, and dicedthe Night Before

1. Spray the pot with cooking spray. 2. Rub the fajita seasoning all over the beef and pork. 3. In the pot, place the meat and cover with lid. 3. Turn dial to SLOW COOK, set temperature to LO, and set time to 10 hours. 4. Transfer the meat to a cutting board and drain the liquid from the pot, saving it for sauces and stocks. Shred the meat using two forks. 5. In the pot, place the shredded meat, cover it with the Green Salsa and poblanos, and cook for 8 hours on low. 6. Use the meat in tostadas, enchiladas, tacos, burritos, or tortas.

Yucatec-Style Roasted Pork

Prep Time: 10 minutes | Cook Time: 8-10 hours | Serves: 6

For the Pork Roast

2 pounds pork butt roast with bone
2 tablespoons achiote paste
½ cup orange juice
¼ cup lime juice
1 tablespoon Mexican oregano
1 teaspoon ground cumin
1 teaspoon smoked paprika
1 teaspoon chili powder

1 teaspoon ground coriander
1 teaspoon chopped garlic
½ teaspoon ground cinnamon
½ teaspoon ground allspice
Pinch salt
Pinch freshly ground black pepper
12 corn tortillas

For the Relish

½ cup grated or finely chopped radishes
¼ cup minced red onion
1 seeded and minced habanero chile pepper
¼ cup orange juice

2 tablespoons lime juice
2 tablespoons water
¼ teaspoon kosher salt
¼ cup chopped cilantro

1. Poke holes all over the pork with a fork. Rub the achiote paste all over the meat. Set aside. 2. In a large bowl, combine together the orange juice with lime juice. Then add in the cumin, paprika, chili powder, garlic, cinnamon, allspice, salt, coriander, and pepper. 3. Submerge the pork in the mixture, cover, and refrigerate overnight. 3. To the pot, add the pork and its overnight marinade. 4. Cover the pot with lid. Turn dial to SLOW COOK, set temperature to LO, and set time to 8 hours. Cook for 8 to 10 hours. The longer it cooks, the more tender it will be. 5. During the last hour of cooking, in a medium bowl, combine together all of the ingredients for the relish. Let stand for at least 10 minute to allow the flavors to blend. 6. When the cooking is over, remove the lid and shred the pork with two forks. 7. To serve, spoon the contents of the pot into tortillas, and top with the relish.

Cheese Meatballs in Tomato Sauce

Prep Time: 20 minutes | Cook Time: 7 hours | Serves: 8

For the Sauce

¼ cup (½ stick) unsalted butter, melted
1 (28-ounce) can diced tomatoes, with juice
1 tablespoon extra-virgin olive oil
2 garlic cloves, minced

2 teaspoons dried basil
1 teaspoon dried parsley
1 teaspoon kosher salt
½ teaspoon freshly ground black pepper

For the Meatballs

2 large eggs
2 cups riced cauliflower
2 cups grated Parmesan cheese, divided
½ cup almond meal
1½ tablespoons Italian seasoning
1 teaspoon kosher salt

½ teaspoon freshly ground black pepper
½ teaspoon garlic powder
1 pound (70% lean) ground beef
12 ounces Italian sausage, casings removed
8 ounces fresh mozzarella cheese, thinly sliced
¼ cup sliced fresh basil leaves

To make the sauce: 1. In the pot, stir together all the ingredients.

To make the meatballs: 1. In a large bowl, beat the eggs, then whisk in the cauliflower, 1 cup of Parmesan cheese, Italian seasoning, salt, almond meal, pepper, and garlic powder. 2. Add the ground beef and sausage and mix well. Form the mixture into 24 (1-inch) balls, placing them in the pot as they are formed. 3. Cover the pot with lid. Turn dial to SLOW COOK, set temperature to LO, and set time to 7 hours. 4. About 15 minutes before serving, scatter the mozzarella cheese over the top of the meatballs and sauce. Cover and continue to cook until the cheese melts, about 15 minutes more. Serve hot, garnished with the remaining 1 cup of Parmesan cheese and the basil leaves.

Italian Stuffed Meatloaf

Prep Time: 10 minutes | Cook Time: 6 hours | Serves: 8

1 pound (70% lean) ground beef
1 pound Italian sausage, casings removed
1 large egg, lightly beaten
1 cup sour cream
½ cup almond meal
½ onion, finely diced
4 garlic cloves, minced
2 tablespoons tomato paste

2 teaspoons dried oregano
1 teaspoon kosher salt
1 teaspoon freshly ground black pepper
1½ cups shredded fontina cheese
½ cup grated Parmesan cheese, divided
½ cup pitted, sliced olives
Extra-virgin olive oil, for coating the aluminum foil

1. In a large bowl, mix the sausage, beef, almond meal, onion, garlic, tomato paste, oregano, salt, egg, sour cream, and pepper. 2. In a separate bowl, toss together the fontina cheese, ¼ cup of Parmesan cheese, and the olives. 3. Lay out a piece of foil large enough to line the pot and create a sling to help you remove the cooked meatloaf. Coat it with olive oil. 4. Form half of the meat mixture into a flat loaf in the center of the foil. Scatter the cheese and olive mixture in a strip down the center of the loaf. Top with the remaining meat mixture, enclosing the cheese and olives in the center of the meatloaf. 5. Sprinkle the remaining ¼ cup of Parmesan over the top. 6. Using the foil sling, lift the loaf and lower it into the pot. 7. Cover the pot with lid. Turn dial to SLOW COOK, set temperature to LO, and set time to 6 hours. Cook for 6 hours on low or 3 hours on high. 8. Use the foil sling to carefully remove the loaf from the pot and transfer to a serving platter. Let the loaf rest for at least 5 minutes before slicing. Serve hot.

Slow-Cooked Shredded Beef

Prep Time: 15 minutes | Cook Time: 8-10 hours | Serves: 10

1 (4-pound) beef butt roast
1 (12-ounce) can or bottle root beer

4 ounces liquid smoke
4 garlic cloves

1. Place the butt roast in the pot and pour the root beer and liquid smoke over the top. Top with the garlic. 2. Cover the pot with lid. Turn dial to SLOW COOK, set temperature to LO, and set time to 8 hours. Cook for 8 to 10 hours. 3. When cooking is complete, transfer the roast to a bowl, then strain the liquid through a fine-mesh sieve, discarding the liquid. 4. Add the softened garlic to the beef and shred the beef using two forks.

Pork Chops with Sweet Potatoes

Prep Time: 10 minutes | Cook Time: 6-8 hours | Serves: 4

1 cup diced onion
4 small sweet potatoes, cut into chunks
1 (10.5-ounce) can low sodium chicken broth (about 1⅓ cups)

1 cup broccoli florets
1 cup sliced carrot
4 boneless, skinless pork chops

1. Layer the onion and sweet potatoes at the bottom of pot. 2. Pour half of the chicken broth over the potatoes and onions. 3. Place the pork chops on top of onions and potatoes, and then top with the broccoli and carrot. Pour the remaining chicken broth on top. 4. Cover the pot with lid. Turn dial to SLOW COOK, set temperature to LO, and set time to 6 hours. Cook for 6 to 8 hours on low or for 3 to 4 hours on high. 5. You can store leftover pork chops in the refrigerator in an airtight container for 3 to 4 days. You can also freeze the cooked meat in an airtight container or heavy-duty freezer bag for 2 to 3 months.

Classic Beef Meatloaf

Prep Time: 10 minutes | Cook Time: 6-8 hours | Serves: 6-8

1 tablespoon extra-virgin olive oil
2 pounds ground beef
1 pound ground pork
1 cup panko or white bread crumbs
1 medium onion, minced
1 tablespoon minced garlic

¼ cup minced fresh parsley
1 teaspoon dried thyme
¾ cup ketchup
2 eggs
1½ teaspoons sea salt
Freshly ground black pepper

1. Coat the interior of the pot with the oil, making sure to cover about two-thirds up the sides of the pot. 2. In a large bowl, combine the ground beef, ground pork, panko, onion, garlic, parsley, thyme, eggs, salt, ketchup, and as much black pepper as desired with your hands until evenly mixed. Spread out the meatloaf mixture in the pot. 3. Cover the pot with lid. Turn dial to SLOW COOK, set temperature to LO, and set time to 6 hours. Cook for 6 to 8 hours or until the meatloaf is cooked through and pulls away from the sides of the pot. 4. When cooking is complete, serve and enjoy.

Sunday Pot Roast with Gravy

Prep Time: 10 minutes | Cook Time: 8-10 hours | Serves: 6

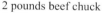

1 (5-pound) chuck roast
2 tablespoons olive oil
2 garlic cloves, minced
1½ teaspoons sea salt
1 tablespoon freshly ground black pepper
1 tablespoon minced fresh rosemary

1 teaspoon minced fresh thyme
1 cup low-sodium beef broth
3 tablespoons dry sherry (optional)
2 tablespoons butter, melted
2 tablespoons all-purpose flour

1. Coat the chuck roast in the oil. In a small bowl, mix together the salt, garlic, rosemary, black pepper, and thyme and rub the mixture all over the roast until well coated. Put the roast in the pot. Add the beef broth and sherry (if using), being careful not to rinse off the seasonings. 2. Cover the pot with lid. Turn dial to SLOW COOK, set temperature to LO, and set time to 8 hours. Cook for 8 to 10 hours. Transfer the roast to a cutting board and let it rest for 10 minutes before cutting into slices. 3. Set temperature to HI. In a small bowl, whisk together butter and flour to make a paste. Place the mixture to the cooking liquid in the pot and whisk until combined. Simmer for another 2 minutes, until the gravy is thickened. Serve the gravy on the side.

Tender Shredded Beef Ragu

Prep Time: 15 minutes | Cook Time: 10 hours | Serves: 6-8

2 pounds beef chuck
1 (28-ounce) can plum tomatoes
1 medium yellow onion, minced
1 carrot, diced
1 celery stalk, diced
6 garlic cloves, peeled and smashed
2 rosemary sprigs, leaves minced

4 thyme sprigs, leaves minced
1 teaspoon sea salt
1 teaspoon freshly ground black pepper
2 cups full-bodied red wine, such as cabernet or Chianti
16 ounces pasta, cooked, for serving
Crunchy artisan bread (optional)

1. Combine the beef, tomatoes, onion, garlic, rosemary, thyme, salt, carrot, celery, black pepper, and wine in the pot. Stir to mix. 2. Cover the pot with lid. Turn dial to SLOW COOK, set temperature to LO, and set time to 10 hours. Cook until the beef is very tender. 3. Using two forks or meat claws, shred the meat. Taste, and adjust the seasoning, if desired. Serve over pasta alongside crunchy artisan bread (if using).

Pork Tenderloin with Peach Sauce

Prep Time: 15 minutes | Cook Time: 5-6 hours | Serves: 6

1 tablespoon canola oil
4 cups peeled sliced peaches
1 tablespoon minced fresh rosemary
1 medium red onion, halved and thinly sliced
1 garlic clove, peeled and smashed
¼ cup balsamic vinegar

½ cup Low-Sodium Chicken Broth, or store-bought
2 (1½-pound) pork tenderloins
Sea salt
Freshly ground black pepper
2 tablespoons brown sugar

1. Coat the interior of the pot with the oil, making sure to cover about two-thirds up the sides of the pot. 2. Spread out the peaches, onion, rosemary, and garlic in the pot. Pour in the vinegar and chicken broth. 3. Place the pork on top of the peach mixture and season generously with black pepper and salt. 4. Cover the pot with lid. Turn dial to SLOW COOK, set temperature to LO, and set time to 5 hours. Cook for 5 to 6 hours until the internal temperature of the meat reaches 145°F. Remove it from the pot and transfer it to a cutting board. Let the meat rest for 15 minutes before cutting it into slices. 5. Stir the brown sugar into the peach sauce, set temperature to HI, and simmer uncovered until the liquid reduces and the sauce is thick and sticky, about 15 minutes. Serve the sauce alongside the pork.

Mediterranean Beef with Pearl Barley

Prep Time: 10 minutes | Cook Time: 8 hours | Serves: 6-8

1 (4-ounce) can tomato paste
½ teaspoon red pepper flakes
2 cups low-sodium beef broth
2 tablespoons extra-virgin olive oil
1 cup dry red wine
1 cup pearl barley

2 pounds beef chuck, cut into 4-inch pieces
Sea salt
Freshly ground black pepper
2 red bell peppers, thinly sliced
1 red onion, halved and thinly sliced

1. Combine the tomato paste, red pepper flakes, olive oil, beef broth, and wine in the pot. Whisk until mixed. Stir in the barley. 2. Lay the beef chuck over the barley and season with black pepper and salt. 3. Spread out the peppers and onion around the beef. 4. Cover the pot with lid. Turn dial to SLOW COOK, set temperature to LO, and set time to 8 hours. Cook until the barley and beef are very tender. 5. When cooking is complete, serve and enjoy.

Traditional Beef Cholent

Prep Time: 10 minutes | Cook Time: 12-26 hours | Serves: 6

½ cup lima beans
½ cup navy beans
1 cup pearl barley
1 small onion, chopped
1 carrot, peeled and cut into 1" pieces
1 pound flanken ribs

2 medium or large potatoes, peeled and cut into large chunks
1 teaspoon sweet paprika
1 teaspoon garlic powder
4 cups water, plus more if needed
2 teaspoons kosher salt
½ teaspoon black pepper

1. Place lima beans, navy beans, and barley in a fine mesh drainer. Rinse several times in cold water and drain. 2. In the pot, place ingredients in the following order: chopped onion, flanken, prepared beans and barley, potatoes, carrot, paprika, garlic powder, and water. 3. Cover the pot with lid. Turn dial to SLOW COOK, set temperature to LO, and set time to 12 hours. Cook for 12 to 26 hours. Check and add water at any time if cholent looks too dry. If there is too much liquid at the end of the cooking time, uncover and let cook for another 30 minutes. Add salt and pepper. Taste and add more salt and pepper if needed. 4. When cooking is complete, serve and enjoy.

Hearty Red Wine Beef Stew
Prep Time: 10 minutes | Cook Time: 8 hours | Serves: 6

⅓ cup red wine
½ cup water
4 red skin potatoes, quartered
3 carrots, cut into thirds
2 bulbs fennel, quartered
2 rutabagas, quartered

1 onion, sliced
4 cloves garlic, sliced
3 pounds beef stew meat, cut into 2" cubes
½ teaspoon kosher salt
½ teaspoon freshly ground black pepper

1. Pour the wine and water into the pot. Add the potatoes, carrots, rutabagas, onion, fennel, and garlic, and stir. 2. Arrange stew meat evenly over vegetables. Sprinkle with pepper and salt. 3. Cover the pot with lid. Turn dial to SLOW COOK, set temperature to LO, and set time to 8 hours. 4. When cooking is complete, serve and enjoy.

Tender Flanken Ribs in Spicy Tomato Sauce
Prep Time: 10 minutes | Cook Time: 6 hours | Serves: 4

2 pounds flanken ribs
1 (28-ounce) can tomato sauce
½ cup water
⅛ cup Worcestershire sauce
2 tablespoons brown sugar
1 teaspoon Tabasco sauce

1 teaspoon salt
¼ teaspoon black pepper
1 lemon, juiced
1 tablespoon soy sauce
¼ cup parsley leaves

1. Add all ingredients except parsley leaves to the pot. 2. Cover the pot with lid. Turn dial to SLOW COOK, set temperature to LO, and set time to 6 hours. 3. When cooking is complete, sprinkle on parsley evenly just before serving.

Slow-Cooked Jerk Pork Chops
Prep Time: 5 minutes | Cook Time: 4-6 hours | Serves: 4

4 (6-ounce) bone-in pork chops, trimmed of fat
1 small onion, sliced
2 garlic cloves, minced
⅓ cup low-sodium chicken broth
1 teaspoon extra-virgin olive oil
1 teaspoon parsley
1 teaspoon dried chopped onion
½ teaspoon garlic powder

½ teaspoon thyme
½ teaspoon salt
½ teaspoon nutmeg
½ teaspoon allspice
½ teaspoon freshly ground black pepper
¼ teaspoon red pepper flakes
¼ teaspoon cayenne pepper
¼ teaspoon cinnamon

1. Place the pork chops, onion, and garlic into the pot. 2. In a small bowl, mix together the broth, olive oil, dried onion, cayenne, garlic powder, thyme, salt, parsley, nutmeg, allspice, black pepper, red pepper flakes, and cinnamon. Pour the mixture over the pork chops. 3. Cover the pot with lid. Turn dial to SLOW COOK, set temperature to LO, and set time to 4 hours. Cook for 4 to 6 hours or on high for 2 to 3 hours. 4. When cooking is complete, serve and enjoy.

Homemade Sephardic Cholent

Prep Time: 10 minutes | Cook Time: 8-12 hours | Serves: 6-8

Cooking spray
2 tablespoons olive oil
2 large onions, chopped
4 cloves garlic, coarsely chopped
3 pounds flanken ribs
2 (15-ounce) cans chickpeas, drained and rinsed
3 large sweet potatoes, peeled and cut into 1" chunks
2 teaspoons ground cumin
1 teaspoon turmeric

1 teaspoon cinnamon
1 tablespoon paprika
½ teaspoon kosher salt
¼ teaspoon black pepper
3 tablespoons honey
Pinch of saffron threads, crushed
1 cup chicken broth
6 uncooked whole eggs

1. Spray the inside of pot with the cooking spray. 2. Heat the oil in a large skillet over medium-high heat. Add the onions and cook, stirring frequently, until they soften and just start to turn brown, about 8 minutes. Add garlic; stir for 30 seconds, then push mixture to the sides. Add flanken and let sear for 3 minutes without disturbing. Carefully turn flanken and sear again for 3 minutes. 3. Transfer flanken and onions into prepared pot and top with chickpeas and sweet potatoes. Sprinkle in the cumin, salt, turmeric, cinnamon, paprika, and pepper. Drizzle in the honey. 4. In a small bowl, mix the saffron into the broth and pour into pot. 5. Nestle the eggs in the center of the pot. 6. Cover the pot with lid. Turn dial to SLOW COOK, set temperature to LO, and set time to 8 hours. Cook for 8 to 12 hours. 7. When cooking is complete, serve and enjoy.

Lamb in Coconut Curry Sauce

Prep Time: 10 minutes | Cook Time: 8-9 hours | Serves: 4

1 tablespoon vegetable oil
1 medium onion, peeled and diced
1 clove garlic, minced
Cooking spray
1 large potato, peeled and diced
2 carrots, peeled and julienned
2 teaspoons curry powder
½ teaspoon ground turmeric
2 teaspoons ground cumin
1 teaspoon cinnamon

1 teaspoon kosher salt
¼ teaspoon ground black pepper
1" piece fresh ginger, peeled and grated (or 1 teaspoon ground ginger)
2 packages (about 3 pounds total) lamb shoulder, cut into 2" pieces
1 (10- to 12-ounce) can coconut milk (regular or light)
1 cup water
2 cups cooked rice, any variety
¼ cup packed coriander leaves

1. Heat the vegetable oil in a large skillet. Add the onion and garlic. Sauté for 5 minutes or until onions just start to brown. Remove from heat and set aside. 2. Spray the inside of pot with cooking spray. Add potato, carrots, onion mixture, and spices; stir to combine. 3. Arrange lamb on top of vegetables. Pour in the coconut milk and the water. 4. Cover the pot with lid. Turn dial to SLOW COOK, set temperature to LO, and set time to 8 hours. Cook for 8 to 9 hours. 5. When cooking is complete, serve the lamb over rice. Ladle the curried sauce over lamb and garnish with cilantro leaves.

Chapter 6 Fish and Seafood

Tuna and Potato Casserole 74

Hearty Salmon Meatloaf............................ 74

Flavorful Salmon Ratatouille 74

Shrimp Scampi with Vegetables 75

Garlic Shrimp and Grits 75

White Fish in Curried Tomato Sauce 75

Monkfish and Sweet Potatoes 76

Cod with Pesto Topping and White Bean Ratatouille 76

Thyme Salmon with Zucchini and Carrot 76

Manhattan Clam Chowder 77

Slow-Cooked Sweet and Sour Scallops 77

Tuna and Potato Casserole

Prep Time: 10 minutes | Cook Time: 7-9 hours | Serves: 5

4 potatoes, peeled
1 tablespoon butter
1 onion, chopped
3 cloves garlic, minced
3 tablespoons flour
1 tablespoon curry powder

½ teaspoon salt
⅛ teaspoon pepper
½ cup heavy cream
½ cup milk
2 stalks celery, chopped
1 (12-ounce) can light tuna, drained

1. Slice potatoes ⅛-inch thick and place in the cold water. 2. Remove the lid from the pot. Turn dial to SEAR/SAUTÉ, set temperature to LO, and press START/STOP to begin preheating. Let the unit preheat for 5 minutes. 3. When preheating is complete, melt the butter in the pot. 4. Add the onion and garlic, cook, and stir for 5 minutes. Add the flour, curry powder, salt, and pepper, and cook until bubbly. 5. Add the heavy cream and milk and bring to a simmer. Drain potatoes thoroughly. Layer potatoes, celery, and tuna in the pot. Pour cream mixture over all. 6. Cover the pot with lid. Turn dial to SLOW COOK, set temperature to LO, and set time to 7 hours. Cook for 7–9 hours until potatoes are tender and casserole is bubbling. 7. When cooking is complete, serve and enjoy.

Hearty Salmon Meatloaf

Prep Time: 10 minutes | Cook Time: 6-7 hours | Serves: 4

⅓ cup brown rice
⅔ cup water
1 tablespoon olive oil
¼ cup finely chopped onion
⅓ cup shredded carrot
¼ cup ground almonds
3 tablespoons flour

2 tablespoons sour cream
½ teaspoon salt
⅛ teaspoon pepper
1 egg
1 (14-ounce) can salmon, drained
¼ cup grated Parmesan cheese
2 tablespoons butter

1. In a small saucepan, combine the rice and water. Bring to a boil, reduce the heat, cover, and simmer for 30 to 40 minutes or until rice is tender and liquid is absorbed. 2. In a large saucepan, heat the olive oil over medium heat. Add onion and carrot, cook, and stir for 4 minutes. Remove from heat and add almonds, flour, salt, sour cream, pepper, and egg. Stir in the cooked rice, then add salmon and cheese and mix. 3. Grease the pot with butter. Form mixture into a loaf that fits into the pot with 1-inch of space all around. Fold two 22-inch long strips of foil into 3" × 22" strips. Place in an "X" position in the bottom of pot, letting ends extend over side. 4. Place loaf in bottom of pot. 5. Cover the pot with lid. Turn dial to SLOW COOK, set temperature to LO, and set time to 6 hours. Cook for 6 to 7 hours or until meatloaf is firm. 6. When cooking is complete, remove from pot using foil strips. Let stand for 5 minutes and slice to serve.

Flavorful Salmon Ratatouille

Prep Time: 20 minutes | Cook Time: 6½-7½ hours | Serves: 8

2 eggplants, peeled and chopped
5 large tomatoes, seeded and chopped
2 cups sliced button mushrooms
2 onions, chopped
2 red bell peppers, stemmed, seeded, and chopped

5 garlic cloves, minced
2 tablespoons olive oil
1 teaspoon dried herbes de Provence
2 pounds salmon fillets

1. In the pot, mix the eggplant, tomatoes, onions, bell peppers, mushrooms, garlic, olive oil, and herbes de Provence. 2. Cover the pot with lid. Turn dial to SLOW COOK, set temperature to LO, and set time to 6 hours. Cook for 6 to 7 hours until the vegetables are tender. 3. Add the salmon to the pot. Cover and cook on low for 30 to 40 minutes until the salmon flakes when tested with a fork. 4. Gently stir the salmon into the vegetables and serve.

Shrimp Scampi with Vegetables

Prep Time: 20 minutes | Cook Time: 5½-7½ hours | Serves: 8

1 pound cremini mushrooms, sliced
2 onions, chopped
2 leeks, chopped
8 garlic cloves, minced
1 cup Fish Stock

¼ cup freshly squeezed lemon juice
1 teaspoon dried basil leaves
2 pounds raw shrimp, shelled and deveined
2 tablespoons butter

1. In the pot, mix the mushrooms, onions, garlic, fish stock, leeks, lemon juice, and basil. 2. Cover the pot with lid. Turn dial to SLOW COOK, set temperature to LO, and set time to 5 hours. Cook for 5 to 7 hours until the vegetables are tender. 3. Stir in the shrimp. Cover again, set temperature to HI, and cook for 30 to 40 minutes, or until the shrimp curl and turn pink. 4. Stir in the butter; cover and let stand for 10 minutes, then serve.

Garlic Shrimp and Grits

Prep Time: 20 minutes | Cook Time: 5½-7½ hours | Serves: 8

2½ cups stone-ground grits
2 onions, chopped
5 garlic cloves, minced
4 large tomatoes, seeded and chopped
2 green bell peppers, stemmed, seeded, and chopped

8 cups Chicken Stock or Roasted Vegetable Broth
1 bay leaf
1 teaspoon Old Bay® Seasoning
2 pounds raw shrimp, peeled and deveined
1½ cups shredded Cheddar cheese

1. In the pot, mix the grits, onions, tomatoes, garlic, bell peppers, bay leaf, chicken stock, and seasoning. 2. Cover the pot with lid. Turn dial to SLOW COOK, set temperature to LO, and set time to 5 hours. Cook for 5 to 7 hours until the grits are tender and most of the liquid is absorbed. 3. Add the shrimp and stir. Cover and cook on low for 30 to 40 minutes longer, or until the shrimp curl and turn pink. 4. Stir in the cheese and serve.

White Fish in Curried Tomato Sauce

Prep Time: 20 minutes | Cook Time: 4½ hours | Serves: 6

2 tablespoons extra-virgin olive oil
1 medium yellow or sweet onion, finely chopped
2 garlic cloves, minced
1 (½-inch) piece fresh ginger, peeled and grated
2 (14½-ounce) cans no-salt-added diced fire-roasted tomatoes, with their juices
¼ teaspoon kosher salt

¼ teaspoon ground black pepper
¼ teaspoon ground cayenne pepper
1 teaspoon curry powder
4 cups stemmed and chopped Tuscan kale
2 pounds firm white fish, such as cod, halibut, or haddock, cut into 3-inch pieces
Fresh chopped parsley, for garnish

1. In the pot, combine the oil, yellow onion, garlic, ginger, salt, tomatoes with their juices, black pepper, cayenne pepper, and curry powder. 2. Cover the pot with lid. Turn dial to SLOW COOK, set temperature to LO, and set time to 3 hours. Cook for 4 hours until hot and bubbly.
3. Add the kale and stir well. Nestle the fish into the sauce. 4. Cover and cook on high for 25 to 30 minutes, until the fish flakes easily with a fork or reaches an internal temperature of 145°F. 5. Spoon into serving bowls and sprinkle with parsley. Serve immediately. 6. Refrigerate the leftovers for up to 4 days or freeze for up to 6 months.

Monkfish and Sweet Potatoes

Prep Time: 10 minutes | Cook Time: 6 hours | Serves: 6

Nonstick cooking spray or olive oil, for greasing
1 cup no-salt-added vegetable broth or chicken stock
1 teaspoon ground cumin
2 medium sweet potatoes, peeled and cut into ½-inch cubes (about 20 ounces)
1 (16-ounce) jar low-sodium salsa verde

1½ pounds monkfish, halibut, cod, or haddock, cut into 2-inch pieces
Sliced green cabbage, for serving
Chopped fresh cilantro, for serving
Plain Greek yogurt, for serving (optional)

1. Grease the pot with nonstick spray or brush with oil. In the pot, combine the broth and cumin. Layer in the sweet potatoes, then pour the salsa on top. 2. Cover the pot with lid. Turn dial to SLOW COOK, set temperature to LO, and set time to 6 hours. Cook for 6 hours until the sweet potatoes are fork-tender. 3. Add the fish to the pot. Cover again, set temperature to HI, and cook for 10 to 15 minutes until the fish flakes easily with a fork or reaches an internal temperature of 145°F. 4. Spoon the fish and sweet potatoes into serving bowls and top with the cabbage, cilantro, and yogurt if using. 5. Refrigerate leftovers for up to 4 days or freeze for up to 3 months.

Cod with Pesto Topping and White Bean Ratatouille

Prep Time: 10 minutes | Cook Time: 6½ hours | Serves: 4

1 tablespoon extra-virgin olive oil
½ medium sweet or yellow onion, finely chopped
2 tablespoons minced garlic
1 (14-ounce) can no-salt-added diced tomatoes, drained
1 pound eggplant, peeled and cut into 1-inch cubes (about 1 medium eggplant)
2 medium zucchini, diced

1½ cups no-salt-added cannellini or other white beans, drained and rinsed
2 tablespoons basil pesto, plus 1 teaspoon
4 (4-ounce) cod fillets
Kosher salt
Freshly ground black pepper

1. In the pot, combine the oil, sweet onion, tomatoes, eggplant, garlic, zucchini, beans, and 1 tablespoon of pesto. 2. Cover the pot with lid. Turn dial to SLOW COOK, set temperature to LO, and set time to 3 hours. Cook for 5 to 6 hours until the eggplant is softened. 3. Brush each cod fillet with 1 teaspoon of pesto. Place the cod on top of the eggplant mixture and cook on low for 25 to 30 minutes until the fish flakes easily with a fork or reaches an internal temperature of 145°F. 4. Serve the cod atop the eggplant mixture. Season with salt and pepper. 5. Refrigerate leftovers for up to 4 days or freeze for up to 3 months.

Thyme Salmon with Zucchini and Carrot

Prep Time: 10 minutes | Cook Time: 2 hours | Serves: 4

1 cup no-salt-added vegetable broth or water
½ cup dry white wine
1 (2-pound) salmon fillet, skin on
1 medium lemon, thinly sliced and seeded
1 medium zucchini, shredded

1 large carrot, shredded
3 or 4 (3-inch) thyme sprigs, plus more for garnish
Kosher salt
Freshly ground black pepper

1. In the pot, pour the broth and wine. Place the salmon, skin-side down, in the pot. Layer the lemon slices on top of the salmon. Evenly distribute the zucchini and carrot on top of the lemon. Add the thyme and season with the pepper and salt. 2. Cover the pot with lid. Turn dial to SLOW COOK, set temperature to LO, and set time to 2 hours. Cook for 2 hours until the salmon flakes easily with a fork or reaches an internal temperature of 145°F. 3. Discard the lemon and thyme and serve the salmon with the zucchini and carrots on top. Garnish with the fresh thyme leaves. 4. Refrigerate leftovers for up to 4 days or freeze for up to 3 months.

Manhattan Clam Chowder
Prep Time: 15 minutes | Cook Time: 8 hours | Serves: 4

½ tablespoon extra-virgin olive oil
½ medium yellow onion, finely chopped
1 large carrot, finely chopped
1 celery rib, finely chopped
½ pound small red potatoes, diced
3 tablespoons chili sauce
1 tablespoon tomato paste
½ tablespoon gluten-free Worcestershire sauce

½ teaspoon dried thyme
½ teaspoon hot sauce
1 (15-ounce) can no-salt-added diced tomatoes, with their juices
1 (8-ounce) bottle clam juice
1 bay leaf
2 (6½-ounce) cans chopped clams, drained
2 tablespoons chopped fresh parsley

1. In the pot, combine the oil, onion, celery, potatoes, carrot, chili sauce, tomato paste, thyme, hot sauce, Worcestershire sauce, tomatoes with their juices, and clam juice. Add the bay leaf. 2. Cover the pot with lid. Turn dial to SLOW COOK, set temperature to LO, and set time to 6 hours. Cook for 6 to 8 hours until the potatoes are fork-tender. 3. Remove and discard the bay leaf and stir in the clams. Cover the pot and let sit for 5 minutes. 4. Ladle into serving bowls and garnish with the parsley. 5. Refrigerate leftovers for up to 4 days or freeze for up to 6 months.

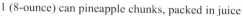

Slow-Cooked Sweet and Sour Scallops
Prep Time: 10 minutes | Cook Time: 4 hours | Serves: 4

1 (8-ounce) can pineapple chunks, packed in juice
¼ cup rice vinegar, white vinegar, or apple cider vinegar
⅓ cup no-salt-added ketchup
1 tablespoon low-sodium gluten-free tamari or soy sauce
1 tablespoon light brown sugar
1 teaspoon minced fresh ginger

1 tablespoon minced garlic
2 medium bell peppers (any color), cut into 1-inch pieces
1 small sweet onion, cut into 1-inch pieces
1 pound sea scallops
Cauliflower rice or brown rice, cooked, for serving (optional)
Thinly sliced scallions, green and white parts, for garnish

1. Drain the pineapple chunks, reserving ¼ cup of the juice. Pour the reserved juice into the pot. Whisk in the vinegar, tamari, brown sugar, ketchup, ginger, and garlic. Add the pineapple chunks, bell peppers, and onion. 2. Cover the pot with lid. Turn dial to SLOW COOK, set temperature to LO, and set time to 4 hours. Cook for 4 hours until the vegetables are crisp-tender. 3. Stir in the scallops. Cover again and cook on low for 8 to 10 minutes, or until the scallops are barely opaque. 4. Divide the rice if using among serving bowls. Top with the scallop mixture and scallions. 5. Refrigerate leftovers for up to 4 days or freeze for up to 3 months.

Chapter 7 Soup, Salad, and Stew

Vegan Black Bean Stew 79

Beef Chili with Black Beans 79

Hot Everything Stew 79

Wild Rice and Vegetable Soup 80

Potato Soup 80

Hearty Beef Stew 80

Tuscan-Style Chicken and White Bean Stew 81

Rosemary Chicken Barley Stew 81

Carrot Barley Soup 81

Smooth Tomato Soup 82

Creamy Zucchini Soup 82

Milky Pumpkin Soup 82

Southwestern Chicken Stew 82

Nutritious Beef Stew 83

Old-Fashioned Vegetable Stew 83

Moroccan Lentil Soup................................. 83

Slow-Cooked Minestrone Soup 84

Slow-Cooked Black Bean Soup 84

Potato and Leek Soup 84

Savory Chicken Fajita Chili 85

Moroccan Lamb Stew with Nuts 85

Mushroom Barley Soup with Flanken 85

Chicken Noodle Soup 86

Beer Cheese Soup 86

Chicken Rice Soup 86

Nutritious Chicken Zoodle Soup 87

No-Bean Chili... 87

Chili Chicken Fajita Soup 87

Limey Chicken Avocado Soup 88

Turkey and Broccoli Slaw Soup.................... 88

Vegan Black Bean Stew

Prep Time: 10 minutes | Cook Time: 7-9 hours | Serves: 4

1 tablespoon olive oil
1 onion, chopped
2 cloves garlic, minced
1 (15-ounce) can black beans, drained
1½ cups frozen corn
1 (10.75-ounce) can

Condensed tomato soup
2 cups Vegetable Broth
2 cups water
¼ teaspoon pepper
1 tablespoon chili powder
½ cup brown rice

1. Remove the lid from the pot. Turn dial to SEAR/SAUTÉ, set temperature to LO, and press START/STOP to begin preheating. Let the unit preheat for 5 minutes. 2. When preheating is complete, heat olive oil in the pot. 3. Add the onion and garlic, cook, and stir until tender, about 6 minutes. Combine with all remaining ingredients in the pot. 3. Cover the pot with lid. Turn dial to SLOW COOK, set temperature to LO, and set time to 7 hours. Cook for 7 to 9 hours or until rice is tender. 4. When cooking is complete, serve immediately.

Beef Chili with Black Beans

Prep Time: 10 minutes | Cook Time: 8-9 hours | Serves: 4

¾ pound round steak
1 tablespoon chili powder
½ teaspoon salt
1 onion, chopped
4 cloves garlic, chopped
1 jalapeño pepper, chopped
⅛ teaspoon cayenne pepper

1 cup tomato juice
1 cup Beef Stock
1 (15-ounce) can black beans, drained
1 (8-ounce) can tomato sauce
1 (16-ounce) jar salsa
1 cup water

1. Cut steak into 1-inch cubes and toss with chili powder and salt. Place onion, garlic, and jalapeño pepper in the pot. 2. Top with beef, cayenne pepper, tomato juice, Stock, black beans, tomato sauce, salsa and water. 3. Cover the pot with lid. Turn dial to SLOW COOK, set temperature to LO, and set time to 9 hours. Cook for 8 to 9 hours until beef is tender. 4. Remove about ⅓ of the beans from the pot, mash, and return to pot. Cook for another 20 to 30 minutes, until mixture is thickened. 5. When cooking is complete, serve and enjoy.

Hot Everything Stew

Prep Time: 10 minutes | Cook Time: 4-5 hours | Serves: 4

2 cups tomato juice
3 cups water
1 cup cooked ground beef or chicken
2 cups cooked vegetables

½ teaspoon hot sauce
3 tablespoons potato flakes
1 cup small pasta
1 cup shredded Cheddar cheese

1. In the pot, combine tomato juice, water, and meat. 2. Cover the pot with lid. Turn dial to SLOW COOK, set temperature to LO, and set time to 4 hours. Cook for 4 to 5 hours until hot. 3. Add remaining ingredients except cheese and cover again. Continue to cook on low for 15 to 20 minutes until stew is thickened and pasta is tender. Stir in cheese, and serve immediately.

Wild Rice and Vegetable Soup

Prep Time: 20 minutes | Cook Time: 7½-9½ hours | Serves: 8

1½ cups wild rice, rinsed and drained
2 onions, chopped
1 leek, chopped
5 garlic cloves, sliced
2 cups sliced cremini mushrooms

4 carrots, peeled and sliced
2 cups frozen corn
8 cups Roasted Vegetable Broth
1 teaspoon dried thyme leaves
2 cups chopped kale

1. In the pot, mix the wild rice, onions, leek, mushrooms, garlic, carrots, and corn. 2. Pour the vegetable broth over all and add the thyme leaves. 3. Cover the pot with lid. Turn dial to SLOW COOK, set temperature to LO, and set time to 7 hours. Cook until the vegetables and wild rice are tender. 4. Stir in the kale. Cover and cook on low for another 20 minutes, or until the kale wilts. 5. When cooking is complete, serve and enjoy.

Potato Soup

Prep Time: 15 minutes | Cook Time: 7½-8 hours | Serves: 10

3 pounds fingerling potatoes, peeled and halved
2 teaspoons minced garlic
1 small white onion, chopped
1½ teaspoons sea salt
½ teaspoon ground black pepper

4 cups Savory Chicken Broth, Savory Vegetable Broth, or store-bought broth
2 cups 2 percent milk
1 cup shredded Cheddar cheese

1. In the pot, combine the potatoes, salt, garlic, onion, black pepper, and broth. 2. Cover the pot with lid. Turn dial to SLOW COOK, set temperature to LO, and set time to 7 hours. Cook for 7 hours until the potatoes are soft. 3. Remove the lid and stir in the milk and cheese. Cover with the lid and cook for another 30 minutes to 1 hour, until the soup is heated through and the cheese has melted. 4. Turn off the pot. Blend the soup until smooth with an immersion blender, b. Pour through a strainer into a separate container, and discard any lumps or bits. Serve warm. 5. Refrigerate leftovers for up to 5 days, or freeze for up to 2 months.

Hearty Beef Stew

Prep Time: 15 minutes | Cook Time: 7½-8 hours | Serves: 8

2 tablespoons extra-virgin olive oil
2 pounds stew beef, cut into 1-inch cubes
Sea salt
Ground black pepper
1 pound fingerling potatoes, peeled and halved (3½ cups)
2 cups baby carrots
1 small onion, diced

3 tablespoons minced garlic
3 cups beef broth
1 (6-ounce) can tomato paste
1 teaspoon dried thyme
⅓ cup potato flakes
Chopped fresh parsley, for garnish (optional)

1. Remove the lid from the pot. Turn dial to SEAR/SAUTÉ, set temperature to HI, and press START/STOP to begin preheating. Let the unit preheat for 5 minutes. 2. When preheating is complete, coat the bottom of pot with the olive oil. 3. Add the beef. Season with black pepper and salt. Sauté for 3 to 4 minutes, until browned. 4. Add the potatoes, onion, carrots, and garlic. Mix well. Stir in the tomato paste, broth, and thyme. Season with black pepper and salt. Mix well. 5. Cover the pot with lid. Turn dial to SLOW COOK, set temperature to LO, and set time to 7 hours. Cook until the vegetables are soft. 6. Remove the lid and stir in the potato flakes. Cover with the lid and cook for another 30 minutes to 1 hour, until thickened. 7. Turn off the pot. Serve the stew warm, garnished with parsley if using. 8. Refrigerate the leftovers for up to 1 week, or freeze for up to 2 months.

Tuscan-Style Chicken and White Bean Stew

Prep Time: 15 minutes | Cook Time: 8 hours | Serves: 6-8

1½ pounds boneless chicken thighs (about 6 whole thighs)
1 pound (3½ cups) halved peeled fingerling or baby potatoes
2 cups baby carrots
1 medium onion, diced
1 cup chopped celery
2 cups chopped kale
2 (15-ounce) cans white cannellini beans, drained and rinsed
1 (14½-ounce) can diced tomatoes, drained
2 tablespoons minced garlic

1 bay leaf
2 teaspoons dried oregano
2 teaspoons dried thyme
2 teaspoons dried rosemary
4 cups Savory Chicken Broth or store-bought chicken broth
Sea salt
Ground black pepper
¾ to 1 cup grated Parmesan cheese, for topping (optional)

1. In the pot, combine the chicken, carrots, onion, potatoes, celery, kale, beans, tomatoes, garlic, bay leaf, thyme, oregano, rosemary, and broth. Mix well. 2. Cover the pot with lid. Turn dial to SLOW COOK, set temperature to LO, and set time to 8 hours. Cook until the chicken has cooked through, the vegetables are soft, and the beans are easily mashed. 3. Remove the lid and remove the chicken. Shred using 2 forks. Return the meat to the pot and stir. Season with the black pepper and salt to taste. 4. Turn off the pot. Discard the bay leaf. Serve the stew warm, topped with 2 tablespoons of cheese per serving if using. 5. Refrigerate leftovers for up to 1 week, or freeze for up to 2 months.

Rosemary Chicken Barley Stew

Prep Time: 20 minutes | Cook Time: 8-10 hours | Serves: 8

2 onions, chopped
4 garlic cloves, minced
4 large carrots, sliced
1¼ cups hulled barley
10 boneless, skinless chicken thighs, cut into 2-inch pieces

1½ cups frozen corn
8 cups Chicken Stock
1 sprig fresh rosemary
1 teaspoon dried thyme leaves
2 cups baby spinach leaves

1. In the pot, mix the onions, carrots, garlic, and barley. Top with the chicken and corn. 2. Pour the chicken stock over all and add the rosemary and thyme leaves. 3. Cover the pot with lid. Turn dial to SLOW COOK, set temperature to LO, and set time to 8 hours. Cook for 8 to 10 hours until the chicken is cooked to 165°F and the barley is tender. 4. Remove and discard the rosemary stem. Stir in the spinach leaves. Cover again, let stand for 5 minutes, and serve.

Carrot Barley Soup

Prep Time: 20 minutes | Cook Time: 8-9 hours | Serves: 8

1½ cups hulled barley
1 bunch (about 6) large carrots, cut into 2-inch chunks and tops reserved
1 large celery root, peeled and cubed
2 onions, chopped
5 garlic cloves, minced

8 cups Roasted Vegetable Broth
2 cups bottled unsweetened carrot juice
1 teaspoon dried dill weed
1 bay leaf
2 tablespoons freshly squeezed lemon juice

1. In the pot, mix the barley, carrots, onions, celery root, and garlic. 2. Add the vegetable broth, carrot juice, dill weed, and bay leaf. 3. Cover the pot with lid. Turn dial to SLOW COOK, set temperature to LO, and set time to 8 hours. Cook for 8 to 9 hours until the barley and vegetables are tender. Remove and discard the bay leaf. 4. Chop the carrot tops and add 1 cup to the pot. Add the lemon juice. Cover and cook on low for another 15 minutes. 5. When cooking is complete, serve and enjoy.

Smooth Tomato Soup

Prep Time: 8 minutes | Cook Time: 6-8 hours | Serves: 8

7 large ripe tomatoes
½ cup raw macadamia nuts
4 cups water or vegetable broth

1 medium onion, chopped
Seasoning: salt, pepper, basil to taste

1. Remove the lid from the pot. Turn dial to SEAR/SAUTÉ, set temperature to LO, and press START/STOP to begin preheating. Let the unit preheat for 5 minutes. 2. When preheating is complete, brown onions for 5 minutes. 3. Add all ingredients to a pot. Cover the pot with lid. Turn dial to SLOW COOK, set temperature to LO, and set time to 6 hours. Cook for 6 to 8 hours. 4. When cooking is complete, using a blender make a smooth purée. Serve warm.

Creamy Zucchini Soup

Prep Time: 5 minutes | Cook Time: 6-8 hours | Serves: 4

3 zucchini, cut in chunks
4 cups vegetable broth
2 Tbsp low fat sour cream

2 cloves garlic, minced
Seasoning: salt, pepper, thyme, basil to taste

1. Combine all ingredients except sour cream in a pot. 2. Cover the pot with lid. Turn dial to SLOW COOK, set temperature to LO, and set time to 6 hours. Cook for 6 to 8 hours. 3. Add sour cream and using a blender make a smooth purée. Serve hot with Parmesan cheese if desired.

Milky Pumpkin Soup

Prep Time: 5 minutes | Cook Time: 6-8 hours | Serves: 4

1 small pumpkin, halved, peeled, seeds removed, pulp cubed
2 cups chicken broth
1 cup coconut milk

Seasonings: salt, pepper, ginger, cinnamon, nutmeg, garlic powder to taste

1. Combine all ingredients in the pot. 2. Close the lid. Cover the pot with lid. Turn dial to SLOW COOK, set temperature to LO, and set time to 6 hours. Cook for 6 to 8 hours. 3. Using a blender make a smooth purée. 4. Decorate with roasted seeds and serve.

Southwestern Chicken Stew

Prep Time: 10 minutes | Cook Time: 8 hours | Serves: 6

2 cups Poultry Broth, or store bought
1 tablespoon cornstarch
1 pound boneless, skinless chicken thighs, cut into 1-inch pieces
2 onions, chopped
3 carrots, peeled and sliced

2 (4-ounce) cans chopped jalapeño peppers, with their juice
2 red bell peppers, seeded and chopped
2 cups fresh or frozen corn
¼ teaspoon sea salt
¼ cup chopped fresh cilantro

1. In a small bowl, whisk together the poultry broth and cornstarch. 2. Add the mixture to the pot, along with the chicken, carrots, jalapeños (and their juice), red bell peppers, onions, corn, and salt. 3. Cover the pot with lid. Turn dial to SLOW COOK, set temperature to LO, and set time to 8 hours. 4. When cooking is complete, stir in the cilantro before serving.

Nutritious Beef Stew

Prep Time: 15 minutes | Cook Time: 8 hours | Serves: 6

2 cups Beef Broth, or store bought
1 tablespoon cornstarch
1 pound stew beef, trimmed and cut into 1-inch cubes
4 slices turkey bacon, browned and crumbled
4 carrots, peeled and chopped
1 pound red potatoes, scrubbed and chopped

1 pound fresh mushrooms, halved
½ cup red wine
1 tablespoon ground mustard
1 teaspoon dried rosemary
¼ teaspoon sea salt
¼ teaspoon freshly ground black pepper

1. In a small bowl, whisk together the broth and cornstarch. 2. Add the mixture to your pot, along with the remaining ingredients. 3. Cover the pot with lid. Turn dial to SLOW COOK, set temperature to LO, and set time to 8 hours. 4. When cooking is complete, skim any excess fat from the surface and discard.

Old-Fashioned Vegetable Stew

Prep Time: 20 minutes | Cook Time: 7-8 hours | Serves: 4-6

⅓ cup chickpea flour
4 red potatoes (about 1⅓ pounds), unpeeled and cut into 1-inch chunks
1 large onion, diced
4 carrots, cut into 1-inch chunks
4 celery stalks, cut into 1-inch chunks
1 pound whole white button or cremini mushrooms
6 cups Low-Sodium Vegetable Broth or store-bought

2 tablespoons Plant-Based Worcestershire Sauce or store-bought
2 tablespoons tomato paste
3 bay leaves
2 teaspoons dried thyme
2 teaspoons garlic powder
Ground black pepper
Salt (optional)

1. Place the chickpea flour and potatoes in a gallon-size resealable bag and shake well to coat. Transfer the floured potatoes to the pot. 2. Add the onion, carrots, celery, mushrooms, broth, tomato paste, bay leaves, thyme, Worcestershire sauce, garlic powder, pepper, and salt if using to the pot and stir to combine. 3. Cover the pot with lid. Turn dial to SLOW COOK, set temperature to LO, and set time to 7 hours. Cook for 7 to 8 hours, stirring occasionally to prevent the stew from sticking. 4. When cooking is complete, remove and discard the bay leaves before serving.

Moroccan Lentil Soup

Prep Time: 15 minutes | Cook Time: 8-10 hours | Serves: 8

2 cups chopped onion
2 cups chopped carrot
1 cup chopped bell pepper
4 garlic cloves, minced
2 teaspoons extra-virgin olive oil
1 teaspoon ground coriander
1 teaspoon ground cumin
1 teaspoon ground turmeric
¼ teaspoon ground cinnamon
¼ teaspoon freshly ground black pepper

6 cups low-sodium vegetable broth
2 cups water
3 cups chopped cauliflower
1¾ cups dry lentils
1 (28-ounce) can no-salt diced tomatoes
4 cups chopped fresh spinach, or 1 (10-ounce) package frozen chopped spinach, thawed
2 tablespoons freshly squeezed lemon juice
Chopped cilantro, for garnish (optional)

1. Combine the onion, carrot, bell pepper, olive oil, coriander, cumin, garlic, turmeric, cinnamon, and black pepper in the pot. Add the broth, water, cauliflower, lentils, and tomatoes, and stir until well combined. 2. Cover the pot with lid. Turn dial to SLOW COOK, set temperature to LO, and set time to 8 hours. Cook for 8 to 10 hours on low or 4 to 5 hours on high until lentils are tender. 3. During the last 30 minutes of cooking, stir in the spinach. Stir in the lemon juice just before serving. 4. Garnish with the chopped cilantro (if using).

Slow-Cooked Minestrone Soup

Prep Time: 5 minutes | Cook Time: 8-10 hours | Serves: 8

1 cup diced celery
1 cup diced carrot
1 cup diced onion
1 cup fresh green beans, cut into 1-inch pieces
64-ounces low-sodium vegetable broth
2 (14.5-ounce) cans no-salt diced tomatoes
1 (15-ounce) can kidney beans, drained and rinsed
1 (15-ounce) can great northern beans, drained and rinsed

4 garlic cloves, minced
1 tablespoon dried basil
2 teaspoons dried oregano
2 teaspoons dried thyme
½ teaspoon dried rosemary, crushed
1 bay leaf
1 teaspoon freshly ground black pepper
1½ cups dried whole wheat elbow pasta

1. Combine all of the ingredients except the pasta in the pot. 2. Cover the pot with lid. Turn dial to SLOW COOK, set temperature to LO, and set time to 8 hours. Cook on low 8 to 10 hours or on high for 4 to 5 hours. Adjust seasonings. 2. Just before serving, turn the pot to high and cook for about 10 minutes. Add the pasta and cook until the pasta is al dente, 10 to 20 minutes. 3. When cooking is complete, serve immediately.

Slow-Cooked Black Bean Soup

Prep Time: 5 minutes | Cook Time: 8 hours | Serves: 8

1 tablespoon extra-virgin olive oil
1 medium yellow onion, chopped
1 red bell pepper, chopped
1 yellow bell pepper, chopped
4 garlic cloves, minced
4 (15-ounce) cans black beans, drained and rinsed

4 cups water
4 cups low-sodium vegetable broth
1 teaspoon ground cumin
¾ teaspoon freshly ground black pepper
½ cup chopped fresh cilantro
Juice of 1 lime, optional

1. Remove the lid from the pot. Turn dial to SEAR/SAUTÉ, set temperature to HI, and press START/STOP to begin preheating. Let the unit preheat for 5 minutes. 2. When preheating is complete, heat the olive oil in the pot. 3. Add the onion and bell peppers and sauté for 4 to 5 minutes until the onion is translucent. 4. Add the garlic and cook until the garlic is fragrant, about 1 minute. 5. Pour the black beans into the pot. Add the water, broth, cumin, and black pepper. Stir to combine the ingredients. 6. Cover the pot with lid. Turn dial to SLOW COOK, set temperature to LO, and set time to 8 hours. Cook for 8 hours on low or 4 hours on high. 7. Once the soup is done, stir in the cilantro and lime juice (if using). Serve warm. 8. Store the cooked soup in the refrigerator in a covered container for 3 to 4 days, or freeze the soup in airtight containers for 4 to 6 months.

Potato and Leek Soup

Prep Time: 10 minutes | Cook Time: 6-8 hours | Serves: 6-8

2 leeks, cleaned and thinly sliced
1 medium yellow onion, thinly sliced
4 medium russet potatoes, peeled and diced
2 garlic cloves, peeled and smashed
2 thyme sprigs, or ½ teaspoon dried thyme

8 cups Low-Sodium Chicken Broth, or store-bought
½ teaspoon sea salt, plus more if desired
½ cup heavy (whipping) cream
Freshly ground black pepper

1. Put the leeks, onion, potatoes, chicken broth, garlic, thyme, and salt into the pot. 2. Cover the pot with lid. Turn dial to SLOW COOK, set temperature to LO, and set time to 6 hours. Cook for 6 to 8 hours. 3. Remove the thyme sprigs and then stir in the cream. 4. Using an immersion blender, puree the soup until smooth or carefully transfer it to a countertop blender and puree until smooth. Taste, and season with more sea salt and black pepper as desired.

Savory Chicken Fajita Chili
Prep Time: 10 minutes | Cook Time: 8 hours | Serves: 6-8

2 pounds boneless skinless chicken thighs
2 green bell peppers, thinly sliced
2 red bell peppers, thinly sliced
2 poblano peppers, thinly sliced
2 medium yellow onions, halved and thinly sliced
1 (15-ounce) can fire-roasted diced tomatoes
2 (15-ounce) cans kidney beans, drained and rinsed
1 tablespoon ancho chili powder

1 teaspoon ground cumin
1 teaspoon smoked paprika
2 corn tortillas, thinly sliced
8 cups Low-Sodium Chicken Broth, or store-bought
Sea salt
Freshly ground black pepper
1 cup sour cream, for serving

1. Put the chicken, green bell peppers, poblano peppers, red bell peppers, onions, tomatoes, beans, ancho chili powder, cumin, corn tortillas, paprika, and chicken broth in the pot. Season generously with black pepper and salt. Stir to mix. 2. Cover the pot with lid. Turn dial to SLOW COOK, set temperature to LO, and set time to 8 hours. 3. Taste and adjust the seasoning, if desired. Serve with sour cream.

Moroccan Lamb Stew with Nuts
Prep Time: 10 minutes | Cook Time: 8-10 hours | Serves: 6-8

2 pounds boneless lamb shoulder, cut into 2-inch cubes
1 medium onion, halved and thinly sliced
1 tablespoon minced ginger
1 tablespoon minced garlic
2 carrots, diced
2 celery stalks, diced
¼ cup white wine
8 cups Low-Sodium Chicken Broth, or store-bought

Zest of one lemon, cut into long strips
2 tablespoons yellow curry powder
1 tablespoon smoked paprika
1 cup pitted green olives, such as Castelvetrano
1 cup roasted almonds
1 cup dried apricots, sliced
1 teaspoon sea salt
1 teaspoon freshly ground black pepper

1. Put the lamb, onion, ginger, celery, white wine, chicken broth, garlic, carrots, lemon zest, curry powder, paprika, olives, salt, almonds, apricots, and black pepper in the pot. Stir to mix. 2. Cover the pot with lid. Turn dial to SLOW COOK, set temperature to LO, and set time to 8 hours. Cook for 8 to 10 hours until the lamb is tender and the stew is very fragrant. 3. Taste and adjust the seasoning, if desired.

Mushroom Barley Soup with Flanken
Prep Time: 10 minutes | Cook Time: 6-8 hours | Serves: 8

1 teaspoon vegetable oil
6 pieces flanken (short ribs)
8 cups water
1 (approx. 6-ounce) cellophane "tube" mushroom-barley

soup mix, any brand
2 medium potatoes, peeled and quartered
1 teaspoon kosher salt, plus more to taste

1. Remove the lid from the pot. Turn dial to SEAR/SAUTÉ, set temperature to HI, and press START/STOP to begin preheating. Let the unit preheat for 5 minutes. 2. When preheating is complete, heat the oil in the pot. Add flanken and brown on all sides, about 2 to 3 minutes per side. 3. Carefully add water and the mushroom-barley soup mix, reserving the small seasoning packet. 4. Cover the pot with lid. Turn dial to SLOW COOK, set temperature to LO, and set time to 6 hours. Cook for 6 to 8 hours. 5. Uncover and add contents of small packet from soup mix along with potatoes. Re-cover and increase the heat to high for 30 minutes. 6. Stir in salt. Taste and add additional salt, if necessary. Ladle soup into bowls and serve. Serve flanken and potatoes as the entrée. 7. Let any remaining soup and flanken stand for 1 hour to cool down, then transfer to a covered pot or casserole; refrigerate for 8 hours or overnight. The following day, peel off and discard congealed layer of fat before reheating.

Chicken Noodle Soup

Prep Time: 10 minutes | Cook Time: 8-10 hours | Serves: 8

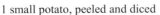

1 small potato, peeled and diced
1 parsnip, cut into chunks
2 carrots, cut lengthwise then thinly sliced
1 small turnip, peeled and diced
1 stalk celery, diced
2 medium onions, cut into chunks
1 whole chicken (3–4 pounds), cut into quarters or eighths, most of skin removed
1 tablespoon fresh thyme leaves

2 teaspoons fresh rosemary leaves, minced
½ teaspoon whole black peppercorns
1 bay leaf
4 sprigs fresh dill
2 sprigs fresh parsley
1 teaspoon kosher salt, plus more to taste
8 cups water
1 (12–16-ounce) bag fine egg noodles

1. Place all ingredients except noodles into the pot in order listed. 2. Cover the pot with lid. Turn dial to SLOW COOK, set temperature to LO, and set time to 8 hours. Cook for 8 to 10 hours. 3. Use a slotted spoon to remove and discard parsley, dill, peppercorns, and bay leaf. 4. Transfer chicken to a cutting board and let cool enough to handle safely. 5. Meanwhile, add noodles to the pot, cover, and continue to cook for an additional 15 to 20 minutes or until noodles are tender. 6. Discard skin of cooled chicken. Remove meat from the chicken bones and dice it; add 2 cups back to pot; freeze remaining diced chicken for future use. Discard bones. 7. Ladle soup into bowls and serve hot.

Beer Cheese Soup

Prep Time: 10 minutes | Cook Time: 4 hours | Serves: 12

½ cup butter or margarine
½ white onion, diced
2 medium carrots, peeled and diced
2 ribs celery, diced
½ cup flour
3 cups Vegetable Broth (see recipe in this chapter)

1 (12-ounce) can or bottle of beer
3 cups milk
3 cups Cheddar cheese
½ teaspoon dry ground mustard
1 teaspoon kosher salt
1 teaspoon black pepper

1. Remove the lid from the pot. Turn dial to SEAR/SAUTÉ, set temperature to HI, and press START/STOP to begin preheating. Let the unit preheat for 5 minutes. 2. When preheating is complete, melt the butter or margarine in the pot. 3. Sauté the onion, carrots, and celery until just softened, about 5 to 7 minutes. 4. Add the flour and stir to form a roux. Let cook for 2 to 3 minutes. 5. In the pot, slowly pour in the broth and beer while whisking. 6. Add the milk, cheese, and dry mustard. 7. Cover the pot with lid. Turn dial to SLOW COOK, set temperature to LO, and set time to 4 hours. 5. Using an immersion blender, blend until smooth. Stir in salt and pepper. Taste and add more if needed.

Chicken Rice Soup

Prep Time: 10 minutes | Cook Time: 7-9 hours | Serves: 8

2 quarts Chicken Stock (see recipe in this chapter)
2 carrots, peeled and diced
2 stalks celery, diced
2-inch piece of fresh ginger, peeled and minced (or 2 teaspoons ground ginger)
1 lime, juiced (about 2 tablespoons)
1 onion, peeled and finely diced

4 cloves garlic, minced
½ teaspoon kosher salt
½ teaspoon freshly ground pepper
½ cup minced cilantro
1½ cups cooked rice, any variety
2 cups diced cooked chicken

1. Place the stock, carrots, celery, ginger, lime juice, garlic, salt, onion, and pepper in the pot. Stir. 2. Cover the pot with lid. Turn dial to SLOW COOK, set temperature to LO, and set time to 7 hours. Cook for 7 to 9 hours. 3. Stir in the cilantro, rice, and chicken. Cook on high for 15 to 30 minutes. 4. Stir prior to serving.

Nutritious Chicken Zoodle Soup

Prep Time: 10 minutes | Cook Time: 4-6 hours | Serves: 4

1 pound boneless, skinless chicken thighs
6 cups low-sodium chicken broth
2 medium zucchini, cut into spaghetti-like strands
2 celery stalks, sliced
2 carrots, peeled and chopped

2 garlic cloves, minced
1 teaspoon cumin
½ teaspoon salt
¼ teaspoon freshly ground black pepper

1. Add the chicken, broth, zucchini, celery, carrots, garlic, salt, cumin, and pepper to the pot. Stir to mix well. 2. Cover the pot with lid. Turn dial to SLOW COOK, set temperature to LO, and set time to 4 hours. Cook on low for 4 to 6 hours or on high for 2 to 3 hours. 3. Remove the chicken from the pot, shred it, toss it back into the soup, and serve.

No-Bean Chili

Prep Time: 10 minutes | Cook Time: 6-8 hours | Serves: 4

1½ pounds 93% lean ground beef
8 ounces tomato paste
1 (15-ounce) can low-sodium or no-salt-added diced tomatoes
1 small onion, chopped
1 bell pepper, seeded and chopped

2 celery stalks, chopped
1½ teaspoons cumin
1½ teaspoons chili powder
½ teaspoon freshly ground black pepper
½ teaspoon salt

1. Add the beef, tomato paste, diced tomatoes, bell pepper, celery, cumin, chili powder, onion, black pepper, and salt to the pot. Stir to mix well. 2. Cover the pot with lid. Turn dial to SLOW COOK, set temperature to LO, and set time to 6 hours. Cook for 6 to 8 hours on low or for 3 to 4 hours on high. 3. When cooking is complete, serve and enjoy.

Chili Chicken Fajita Soup

Prep Time: 10 minutes | Cook Time: 6-8 hours | Serves: 4

2 pounds boneless, skinless chicken thighs
2 bell peppers, seeded and sliced
1 onion, sliced
1 (28-ounce) can low-sodium or no-salt-added diced tomatoes
2 teaspoons chili powder
1 teaspoon ground cumin

½ teaspoon paprika
½ teaspoon salt
½ teaspoon freshly ground black pepper
⅛ teaspoon garlic powder
⅛ teaspoon onion powder
⅛ teaspoon oregano
⅛ teaspoon red pepper flakes

1. Add the chicken, bell peppers, onion, chili powder, cumin, paprika, salt, tomatoes, black pepper, oregano, garlic powder, onion powder, and red pepper flakes to the pot. Stir to mix well. 2. Cover the pot with lid. Turn dial to SLOW COOK, set temperature to LO, and set time to 6 hours. Cook for 6 to 8 hours on low or for 3 to 4 hours on high. 3. When cooking is complete, serve and enjoy.

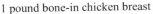

Limey Chicken Avocado Soup

Prep Time: 5 minutes | Cook Time: 4-6 hours | Serves: 6

1 pound bone-in chicken breast
8 cups low-sodium chicken broth
2 scallions (whites and greens), sliced
1 tomato, diced
1 celery stalk, sliced
2 garlic cloves, minced
¼ teaspoon cumin

1 teaspoon salt
1 teaspoon freshly ground black pepper
1 tablespoon freshly squeezed lime juice
¼ cup chopped fresh cilantro, plus additional whole cilantro leaves for garnish
2 avocados, sliced
Lime wedges, for garnish

1. Add the chicken, broth, scallions, celery, garlic, cumin, salt, tomato, pepper, lime juice, and cilantro to the pot. 2. Cover the pot with lid. Turn dial to SLOW COOK, set temperature to LO, and set time to 4 hours. Cook on low for 4 to 6 hours or on high for 2 to 3 hours. 3. Remove the chicken, shred the meat from the bones, and add the shredded meat back into the pot. Stir to combine. 4. Ladle into 6 bowls and top with avocado slices. 5. Serve with the lime wedges on the side.

Turkey and Broccoli Slaw Soup

Prep Time: 5 minutes | Cook Time: 6-8 hours | Serves: 6

1 pound 93% lean ground turkey
1 (12-ounce) package broccoli slaw
4 cups Chicken Stock
  1 (15-ounce) can low-sodium or no-salt-added diced tomatoes
  1 small onion, diced
  2 garlic cloves, minced

1 tablespoon Italian seasoning
1 teaspoon salt
½ teaspoon freshly ground black pepper
Handful chopped fresh parsley for garnish (optional)

1. Add the turkey, broccoli slaw, stock, onion, garlic, Italian seasoning, salt, tomatoes, and pepper to the pot. Stir to mix well. 2. Cover the pot with lid. Turn dial to SLOW COOK, set temperature to LO, and set time to 6 hours. Cook for 6 to 8 hours on low or for 3 to 4 hours on high. 3. When cooking is complete, garnish with the parsley, if using.

Chapter 8 Desserts

Vanilla Coconut Yogurt 90

Apple and Pear Compote with Cranberries 90

Chocolate Chip Lava Cake 90

Apple & Peach Crumble 91

Mixed Berry Crisp 91

Peach Brown Betty with Cranberries 91

Cinnamon Carrot Pudding 92

Banana-Pineapple Foster 92

Cheesy Raspberry Cookies 92

Lemon Butter Cake 93

Comforting Maple Banana Sundaes 93

Vanilla Lemon Custard 93

Golden Almond Cake 94

Mouthwatering Lemon Poppy Seed Cake 94

Yummy Pumpkin Spice Pudding 95

Coconut Chai Custard 95

Minty Chocolate Truffles 95

Simple Banana Cream Pie 96

Tasty Peanut Butter Chocolate Cake 96

Spiced Rum-Raisin Rice Pudding 96

Delicious Chocolate Lava Cake 97

Rich Sabra Compote 97

Rice Pudding with Raisins 97

Sweet Strawberry Pandowdy 98

Homemade Rocky Road Candy 98

Flavorful Double Chocolate Brownies 98

Fluffy Blueberry Muffin Cake....................... 99

Fresh Strawberry Cobbler 99

Light Crustless Pumpkin Pie 99

Vanilla Coconut Yogurt

Prep Time: 15 minutes | Cook Time: 1-2 hours | Serves: 3-4

3 (13.5-ounce) cans full-fat coconut milk
5 probiotic capsules (not pills)

1 teaspoon raw honey
½ teaspoon vanilla extract

1. Pour the coconut milk into the pot. 2. Cover the pot with lid. Turn dial to SLOW COOK, set temperature to HI, and set time to 1 hours. Cook for 1 to 2 hours until the temperature of the milk reaches 180°f measured with a candy thermometer. 3. Turn off the pot and allow the temperature of the milk to come down close to 100°f. 4. Open the probiotic capsules and pour in the contents, along with the honey and vanilla. Stir well to combine. 5. Recover the pot, turn it off and unplug it, and wrap it in an insulating towel to keep warm overnight as it ferments. 6. Pour the yogurt into sterilized jars and refrigerate. The yogurt should thicken slightly in the refrigerator, where it will keep for up to 1 week.

Apple and Pear Compote with Cranberries

Prep Time: 10 minutes | Cook Time: 6-8 hours | Serves: 4-6

¾ cup no-sugar-added cranberry juice
¼ cup pure maple syrup
2 medium apples, peeled, cored, and chopped

2 medium pears, peeled, cored, and chopped
⅓ cup dried cranberries
1 to 1½ cups no-sugar-added vanilla ice cream (optional)

1. In the pot, combine the cranberry juice, apples, pears, maple syrup, and dried cranberries. 2. Cover the pot with lid. Turn dial to SLOW COOK, set temperature to LO, and set time to 6 hours. Cook for 6 to 8 hours until the apples and pears are soft and easily mashed. 3. When cooking is complete, serve the compote warm on its own or with ¼ cup of ice cream per serving. 4 Refrigerate the leftovers for up to 5 days, or freeze for up to 1 month.

Chocolate Chip Lava Cake

Prep Time: 15 minutes | Cook Time: 4-5 hours | Serves: 10-12

1 tablespoon coconut oil, plus ½ cup
1 (16-ounce) box sugar-free devil's food cake mix, such as Pillsbury
1¼ cups 2 percent milk, plus 2 cups
3 large eggs
1 (4-ounce) box sugar-free instant chocolate pudding mix,

such as Jell-O or Royal brands
¾ cup coconut sugar
1 (12-ounce) bag semisweet chocolate chips
2½ to 3 cups no-sugar-added vanilla ice cream (optional)
1¼ to 1½ cups light whipped cream, for topping (optional)

1. Coat the bottom and sides of pot with 1 tablespoon of coconut oil. 2. For the cake batter, in a large bowl, beat together 1¼ cups of milk, the cake mix, the remaining ½ cup of coconut oil, and the eggs until thoroughly combined. 3. Pour the cake batter into the pot in an even layer. 4. For the topping, in a medium bowl, combine the pudding mix, sugar, and 2 cups of milk. 5. Pour the topping over the cake batter. Do not stir. 6. Sprinkle the chocolate chips over the topping. 7. Cover the pot with lid. Turn dial to SLOW COOK, set temperature to LO, and set time to 4 hours. Cook for 4 to 5 hours until the top is spongy and the inside is gooey. 8. When cooking is complete, serve the cake warm with ¼ cup of ice cream per serving if using or 2 tablespoons of light whipped cream per serving if using. 9. Refrigerate leftovers for up to 5 days, or freeze for up to 2 months.

Apple & Peach Crumble

Prep Time: 20 minutes | Cook Time: 4-5 hours | Serves: 8

6 large Granny Smith apples, peeled and cut into chunks
4 large peaches, peeled and sliced
3 tablespoons honey
2 tablespoons lemon juice
1 cup almond flour

1 teaspoon ground cinnamon
3 cups quick-cooking oatmeal
⅓ cup coconut sugar
½ cup slivered almonds
½ cup coconut oil, melted

1. In the pot, mix the apples, honey, peaches, and lemon juice. 2. In a large bowl, mix the oatmeal, almond flour, coconut sugar, cinnamon, and almonds until well combined. 3. Add the coconut oil and mix until crumbly. 4. Sprinkle the almond mixture over the fruit in the pot. 5. Cover the pot with lid. Turn dial to SLOW COOK, set temperature to LO, and set time to 4 hours. Cook for 4 to 5 hours until the fruit is tender and the crumble is bubbling around the edges. 6. When cooking is complete, serve and enjoy.

Mixed Berry Crisp

Prep Time: 20 minutes | Cook Time: 5-6 hours | Serves: 12

3 cups frozen organic blueberries
3 cups frozen organic raspberries
3 cups frozen organic strawberries
2 tablespoons lemon juice
2½ cups rolled oats

1 cup whole-wheat flour
⅓ cup maple sugar
1 teaspoon ground cinnamon
⅓ cup coconut oil, melted

1. Do not thaw the berries. In the pot, mix the frozen berries. Drizzle with the lemon juice. 2. In a large bowl, mix the oats, maple sugar, flour, and cinnamon until well combined. Stir in the melted coconut oil until crumbly. 3. Sprinkle the oat mixture over the fruit in the pot. 4. Cover the pot with lid. Turn dial to SLOW COOK, set temperature to LO, and set time to 5 hours. Cook for 5 to 6 hours until the fruit is bubbling and the topping is browned. 5. When cooking is complete, serve and enjoy.

Peach Brown Betty with Cranberries

Prep Time: 20 minutes | Cook Time: 5-6 hours | Serves: 10

8 ripe peaches, peeled and cut into chunks
1 cup dried cranberries
2 tablespoons freshly squeezed lemon juice
3 tablespoons honey
3 cups cubed whole-wheat bread

1½ cups whole-wheat bread crumbs
⅓ cup coconut sugar
¼ teaspoon ground cardamom
⅓ cup melted coconut oil

1. In the pot, mix the peaches, lemon juice, dried cranberries, and honey. 2. In a large bowl, mix the coconut sugar, bread crumbs, bread cubes, and cardamom. Drizzle the melted coconut oil over all and toss to coat. 3. Sprinkle the bread mixture on the fruit in the pot. 4. Cover the pot with lid. Turn dial to SLOW COOK, set temperature to LO, and set time to 5 hours. Cook for 5 to 6 hours until the fruit is bubbling and the topping is browned. 5. When cooking is complete, serve and enjoy.

Cinnamon Carrot Pudding

Prep Time: 20 minutes | Cook Time: 5-7 hours | Serves: 12

3 cups finely grated carrots
1½ cups chopped pecans
1 cup golden raisins
1 cup almond flour
1 cup coconut flour

½ cup coconut sugar
1 teaspoon baking powder
1½ teaspoons ground cinnamon
2 eggs, beaten
2 cups canned coconut milk

1. In the pot, mix all of the ingredients. 2. Cover the pot with lid. Turn dial to SLOW COOK, set temperature to LO, and set time to 5 hours. Cook for 5 to 7 hours until the pudding is set. 3. When cooking is complete, serve warm, either plain or with softly whipped heavy cream.

Banana-Pineapple Foster

Prep Time: 10 minutes | Cook Time: 1 hour 15 minutes | Serves: 7

½ cup dark brown sugar
3 Tbsp butter, cut into pieces
¼ cup light unsweetened coconut milk
1 cup fresh pineapples, cubed

4 ripe bananas, cut into ½-inch-thick slices
1¾ cups vanilla reduced-fat ice cream
¼ tsp ground cinnamon
¼ cup dark rum

1. Spray the pot with cooking spray. 2. In the pot, stir together the brown sugar, coconut milk, butter, and rum. 3. Cover the pot with lid. Turn dial to SLOW COOK, set temperature to LO, and set time to 1 hour. 4. Whisking makes a smooth mixture. Coat the pineapples, cinnamon and bananas in the sauce. 5. Cover and cook 15 minutes longer. 6. When cooking is complete, serve warm with ice cream.

Cheesy Raspberry Cookies

Prep Time: 5 minutes | Cook Time: 4 hours | Serves: 8

1 egg
1 cup almond flour
4 oz cream cheese, softened

1 oz raspberries
6 Tbsp erythritol, powdered

1. Using a blender, mix together 2 oz cheese cream, an egg, 4 Tbsp erythritol and flour. 2. To make the filling, blend 2 oz cheese cream with 1 Tbsp erythritol. 3. In a separate bowl, blend 1 Tbsp erythritol with raspberries. 4. Cover the pot bottom with a foil sheet. Using a spoon scoop the batter onto it making small cookies. Make a hollow in the center of each cookie and fill them with the cream cheese mixture followed by raspberries. 5. Cover the pot with lid. Turn dial to SLOW COOK, set temperature to LO, and set time to 4 hours. 6. When cooking is complete, serve and enjoy.

Lemon Butter Cake

Prep Time: 15 minutes | Cook Time: 3 hours | Serves: 6-8

2 eggs
2 cups almond flour
Zest from 2 lemons

½ cup melted butter
6 Tbsp Swerve

1. In a medium bowl, combine the flour with sweetener. 2. In another bowl, whisk together eggs, butter, and lemon zest. 3. Combine dry and wet mixtures and blend well. 4. Cover the pot bottom with foil and spread the batter. 5. Cover the pot with lid. Turn dial to SLOW COOK, set temperature to HI, and set time to 3 hours. 6. When cooking is complete, serve and enjoy.

Comforting Maple Banana Sundaes

Prep Time: 10 minutes | Cook Time: 2 hours | Serves: 6

Nonstick cooking spray
4 bananas, peeled, halved crosswise, and then halved lengthwise
2 tablespoons chopped unsalted pecans
½ cup pure maple syrup

1 teaspoon rum extract
1 tablespoon unsalted butter, melted
Zest and juice of 1 orange
Pinch sea salt
6 scoops low-fat vanilla ice cream or frozen yogurt

1. Spray the pot with nonstick cooking spray. 2. Put the bananas and unsalted pecans in the bottom of the pot. 3. In a small bowl, whisk together the butter, orange zest and juice, maple syrup, rum extract, and salt. Pour the syrup mixture over the bananas and pecans. 4. Cover the pot with lid. Turn dial to SLOW COOK, set temperature to LO, and set time to 2 hours. 5. When cooking is complete, to serve, spoon the bananas, pecans, and syrup over the ice cream.

Vanilla Lemon Custard

Prep Time: 10 minutes | Cook Time: 3 hours | Serves: 4

5 egg yolks
¼ cup freshly squeezed lemon juice
1 tablespoon lemon zest
1 teaspoon pure vanilla extract

⅓ teaspoon liquid stevia
2 cups heavy (whipping) cream
1 cup whipped coconut cream

1. In a medium bowl, whip together the yolks, vanilla, lemon juice and zest, and liquid stevia. 2. Whisk in the heavy cream and divide the mixture between 4 (4-ounce) ramekins. 3. Place a rack that fits your pot at the bottom of the pot and place the ramekins on it. 4. Pour in enough water to reach halfway up the sides of the ramekins. 5. Cover the pot with lid. Turn dial to SLOW COOK, set temperature to LO, and set time to 3 hours. 6. Remove the ramekins from the pot and cool to room temperature. 7. Chill the ramekins completely in the refrigerator and serve topped with whipped coconut cream.

Golden Almond Cake
Prep Time: 15 minutes | Cook Time: 3 hours | Serves: 8

½ cup coconut oil, divided
1½ cups almond flour
½ cup coconut flour
½ cup granulated erythritol
2 teaspoons baking powder

3 eggs
½ cup coconut milk
2 teaspoons pure vanilla extract
½ teaspoon almond extract

1. Line the pot with aluminum foil and grease the aluminum foil with 1 tablespoon of the coconut oil. 2. In a medium bowl, mix the erythritol, coconut flour, almond flour, and baking powder. 3. In a large bowl, whisk together the remaining coconut oil, coconut milk, vanilla, eggs, and almond extract. 4. Pour the dry ingredients into the wet ingredients and stir until well blended. 5. Transfer the batter to the pot and use a spatula to even the top. 6. Cover the pot with lid. Turn dial to SLOW COOK, set temperature to LO, and set time to 3 hours. Cook until a toothpick inserted in the center comes out clean. 7. When cooking is complete, remove the cake from the pot and cool completely before serving.

Mouthwatering Lemon Poppy Seed Cake
Prep Time: 15 minutes | Cook Time: 2-2½ hours | Serves: 6-8

For the Cake
Nonstick cooking spray (optional)
1 cup rolled oats, blended into flour
1 cup white whole-wheat flour
1 teaspoon baking powder
½ teaspoon baking soda
¼ teaspoon ground turmeric
⅓ cup maple syrup
For the Glaze
3 tablespoons unsweetened shredded coconut
3 tablespoons unsweetened plant-based milk
2 tablespoons maple syrup or Date Syrup

½ cup unsweetened plant-based milk
Zest of 1 lemon (about 1 tablespoon)
⅓ cup lemon juice
3 tablespoons aquafaba
1½ teaspoons apple cider vinegar
1½ teaspoons poppy seeds

1 teaspoon lemon zest
Juice from ½ lemon (about 2 teaspoons)

1. Prepare the pot by folding two long sheets of aluminum foil and placing them perpendicular to each other (crisscross) in the bottom of the pot to create "handles" that will come out over the top of the pot. Coat the inside of the pot and the foil with cooking spray if using or line it with a pot liner. 2. To make the cake: in a large bowl, stir together the oat flour, whole-wheat flour, baking soda, baking powder, and turmeric. Set aside. 3. In a medium bowl, whisk together the milk, lemon juice, maple syrup, aquafaba, lemon zest, and vinegar. Stir in the poppy seeds. Add the milk mixture into the flour mixture and stir well with a wooden spoon. You will notice a little foaming. That is the acid from the lemons and vinegar reacting with the baking powder and is what will give the cake a nice lift and tang. 4. To keep the condensation that forms on the inside of the lid away from the cake as it bakes, stretch a clean dish towel or several layers of paper towels across the top of the slow cooker, but not touching the food, and place the lid on top of the towel(s). If you skip this step, you will have a soggy result. 5. Cover the pot with lid. Turn dial to SLOW COOK, set temperature to HI, and set time to 2 hours. Cook for 2 to 2½ hours. To test for doneness, insert a toothpick into the center of the cake; when it comes out clean, the cake is done. Remove the pot and allow the cake to cool for at least 30 minutes before removing the cake from the pot. 6. To make the glaze: When the cake is cool, put the coconut in a food processor or blender and process until smooth, scraping down the sides as needed. Add the milk, syrup, lemon zest, and lemon juice and blend until smooth. Pour over the cake and serve immediately.

Yummy Pumpkin Spice Pudding

Prep Time: 5 minutes | Cook Time: 8 hours | Serves: 10

3 tablespoons melted coconut oil, plus more for coating the pot
2 cups canned coconut milk
1½ cups puréed pumpkin
4 large eggs, lightly beaten
1 tablespoon pure vanilla extract

½ cup erythritol
¼ cup almond flour
2 teaspoons pumpkin pie spice
1 teaspoon stevia powder
1 teaspoon baking powder

1. Generously coat the inside of the pot with coconut oil. 2. In the pot, stir together 3 tablespoons of coconut oil, coconut milk, eggs, vanilla, erythritol, almond flour, pumpkin, pumpkin pie spice, stevia powder, and baking powder until smooth. 3. Cover the pot with lid. Turn dial to SLOW COOK, set temperature to LO, and set time to 8 hours. 4. When cooking is complete, serve warm or refrigerate for up to 3 days and serve chilled.

Coconut Chai Custard

Prep Time: 10 minutes | Cook Time: 5 hours | Serves: 8

4 cups canned coconut milk
4 chai tea bags
1 tablespoon coconut oil
8 large eggs, lightly beaten

1 cup erythritol or 1 teaspoon stevia powder
2 teaspoons stevia powder
1 teaspoon pure vanilla extract or vanilla bean paste

1. Remove the lid from the pot. Turn dial to SEAR/SAUTÉ, set temperature to HI, and press START/STOP to begin preheating. Let the unit preheat for 5 minutes. 2. When preheating is complete, heat the coconut milk in the pot until it simmers. 3. Remove from the heat and add the tea bags. Steep for 5 to 10 minutes. Remove and discard the tea bags and clean the pot. 4. Generously coat the inside of the pot with the coconut oil. 5. In the pot, stir together the tea-infused coconut milk, eggs, stevia powder, erythritol, and vanilla until well combined. 6. Cover the pot with lid. Turn dial to SLOW COOK, set temperature to LO, and set time to 5 hours. 7. Turn off the pot and let cool in the pot for 1 to 2 hours. 8. Serve immediately or refrigerate for up to 3 days and serve chilled.

Minty Chocolate Truffles

Prep Time: 45 minutes | Cook Time: 5 hours | Serves: 10

14 ounces semisweet chocolate, coarsely chopped
¾ cup half-and-half
½ teaspoon pure vanilla extract

1½ teaspoon peppermint extract
2 tablespoons unsalted butter, softened
¾ cup naturally unsweetened or Dutch-process cocoa powder

1. Place semisweet chocolate in a large heatproof bowl. 2. Microwave in four 15-second increments, stirring after each, for a total of 60 seconds. Stir until almost completely melted. Set aside. 3. Remove the lid from the pot. Turn dial to SEAR/SAUTÉ, set temperature to HI, and press START/STOP to begin preheating. Let the unit preheat for 5 minutes. 4. When preheating is complete, heat the half-and-half in the pot, whisking occasionally, until it just becomes to boil. Remove from the heat and then whisk in the vanilla and peppermint extracts. 5. Pour the mixture over the chocolate and, using a wooden spoon, gently stir in one direction. 6. When the chocolate and cream are smooth, stir in the butter until it is combined and melted. 7. Cover with plastic wrap pressed on the top of the mixture, then let it sit at room temperature for 30 minutes. 8. After 30 minutes, place the mixture in the refrigerator until it is thick and can hold a ball shape, about 5 hours. 9. Line a large baking sheet with parchment paper or a use a silicone baking mat. Set aside. 10. Remove the mixture from the refrigerator. Place the cocoa powder in a bowl. 11. Scoop 1 teaspoon of the ganache and, using your hands, roll into a ball. Roll the ball in the cocoa powder, the place on the prepared baking sheet. You can coat your palms with a little cocoa powder to prevent sticking. 12. Serve immediately or cover and store at room temperature for up to 1 week.

Simple Banana Cream Pie

Prep Time: 10 minutes | Cook Time: 5 minutes | Serves: 8

3 cups whole milk
¾ cup white sugar
⅓ cup all-purpose flour
3 egg yolks, slightly beaten, or Egg Beaters

2 tablespoons unsalted butter
1 teaspoon vanilla
3 bananas
1 (9-inch) prebaked pie crust

1. In a large saucepan, scald the milk. 2. Remove the lid from the pot. Turn dial to SEAR/SAUTÉ, set temperature to HI, and press START/STOP to begin preheating. Let the unit preheat for 5 minutes. 3. When preheating is complete, combine the sugar and flour in the pot. Gradually stir in the scalded milk, whisking constantly, and cook until thickened. 4. Cover and cook for 2 minutes more, stirring occasionally. 5. Stir ¼ cup of the hot sugar-milk mixture into the beaten egg yolks. When thoroughly combined, stir the yolk mixture into the remaining sugar-milk mixture. Cook for 1 minute more, stirring constantly. 6. Remove from the heat and blend in the butter and vanilla. Let the pie sit until it's cool. 7. When cool, slice the bananas and scatter on the pie crust. Pour the lukewarm sugar-milk mixture over the bananas. Wait until the pie is cool before serving, or refrigerate overnight for at least 6 hours.

Tasty Peanut Butter Chocolate Cake

Prep Time: 10 minutes | Cook Time: 3 hours | Serves: 6-8

1 tablespoon butter
1 box chocolate cake mix
3 eggs
½ cup oil

1¼ cups water
1 cup butterscotch chips
1 cup creamy peanut butter
½ cup milk

1. Coat the interior of the pot with the butter, making sure to cover about two-thirds up the sides of the pot. 2. In a separate bowl, whisk together the cake mix, oil, eggs, and water. Pour the mixture into the pot. 3. Sprinkle the butterscotch chips over the surface of the cake batter. 4. In the same bowl you used to mix the cake batter, combine the peanut butter and milk. 5. Top the cake batter with spoonfuls of the peanut butter mixture, dropping each spoonful a few inches apart. Use a knife to swirl the peanut butter mixture, incorporating the butterscotch chips as you go. Make sure not to thoroughly mix. You still want a distinct peanut butter swirl. 6. Cover the pot with lid. Turn dial to SLOW COOK, set temperature to LO, and set time to 3 hours. Cook until set. 7. When cooking is complete, serve and enjoy.

Spiced Rum-Raisin Rice Pudding

Prep Time: 5 minutes | Cook Time: 4 hours | Serves: 8

1 tablespoon vegan butter or regular butter
2 cups short-grain white rice
2 teaspoons ground cinnamon
2 (14-ounce) cans full-fat coconut milk, plus more if desired
¼ cup spiced dark rum

¾ cup brown sugar
¼ teaspoon sea salt
1 tablespoon vanilla extract
1 cup raisins
1 cup water

1. Coat the interior of the pot with the butter, making sure to cover about two-thirds up the sides of the pot. 2. Put the rice, cinnamon, rum, brown sugar, salt, coconut milk, vanilla, raisins, and water in the pot. Stir gently to mix. 3. Cover the pot with lid. Turn dial to SLOW COOK, set temperature to LO, and set time to 4 hours. Cook until the rice is tender. 4. Stir in additional coconut milk or water to thin the pudding to your desired consistency. 5. When cooking is complete, serve and enjoy.

Delicious Chocolate Lava Cake

Prep Time: 10 minutes | Cook Time: 3½ hours | Serves: 8-10

1 tablespoon butter
1 box chocolate cake mix
3 eggs
½ cup oil
2 teaspoons vanilla extract

1½ cups water
1 (4-ounce) package instant chocolate pudding mix
2 cups whole milk
1 tablespoon instant coffee powder (optional)
1 (11-ounce) bag 60 percent cacao chocolate chips

1. Coat the interior of the pot with the butter, making sure to cover about two-thirds up the sides of the pot. 2. In a large bowl, whisk together the oil, cake mix, vanilla, eggs, and water. Pour the mixture into the pot. 3. In the same bowl you used to mix the cake batter, whisk together the pudding mix, milk, and instant coffee powder. Pour this mixture over the chocolate cake mix. Top with the chocolate chips. 4. Cover the pot with lid. Turn dial to SLOW COOK, set temperature to HI, and set time to 3½ hours. Cook until set in the center. 5. When cooking is complete, serve and enjoy.

Rich Sabra Compote

Prep Time: 10 minutes | Cook Time: 3-4 hours | Serves: 8

1 (15-ounce) can sliced peaches, drained
1 (15-ounce) can dark sweet cherries, drained
1 (15-ounce) can pear halves, drained
1 (15-ounce) can apricot halves, drained
½ cup mixture dates and dried plums (prunes)

¼ cup light brown sugar, packed
¼ cup orange juice
2 tablespoons Sabra liqueur
½ teaspoon cinnamon
¼ teaspoon ground ginger

1. Place all ingredients in the pot. 2. Cover the pot with lid. Turn dial to SLOW COOK, set temperature to LO, and set time to 3 hours. Cook for 3 to 4 hours. 3. When cooking is complete, serve warm or chilled.

Rice Pudding with Raisins

Prep Time: 10 minutes | Cook Time: 3 hours | Serves: 8

Cooking spray
2 eggs, lightly beaten
⅓ cup granulated sugar
1 teaspoon vanilla extract
¼ teaspoon kosher salt
1 (12-ounce) can evaporated milk (regular, low-fat, or fat-

free)
2 tablespoons unsalted butter, melted
2 cups cooked long-grain rice
½ cup raisins
½ teaspoon ground cinnamon
2 cups Cherry Sauce (see recipe in this chapter), warmed

1. Spray the inside of pot with cooking spray. 2. Combine remaining ingredients except cinnamon and cherry sauce in the pot, and mix well. 3. Cover the pot with lid. Turn dial to SLOW COOK, set temperature to HI, and set time to 1 hour. 4. Sprinkle cinnamon evenly over surface, then re-cover and cook on low for 2 more hours or on high for 1 more hours. 5. Turn off pot. Let stand, covered, for a half hour to let pudding firm up. 6. To serve, divide rice pudding among 8 serving bowls. Ladle cherry sauce over pudding. Serve warm.

Sweet Strawberry Pandowdy

Prep Time: 10 minutes | Cook Time: 1½ hours | Serves: 4

4 cups whole strawberries, stems removed
½ teaspoon ground ginger
1½ tablespoons sugar
½ teaspoon cornstarch

¾ cup flour
3 tablespoons cold unsalted butter, cubed
3 tablespoons cold water
⅛ teaspoon table salt

1. Place the strawberries, ginger, sugar, and cornstarch into the pot. Toss to distribute evenly. 2. Place the flour, butter, water, and salt into a food processor. Mix until a solid ball of dough forms. Roll it out on a clean surface until it is about ¼"–½" thick and will completely cover the fruit in the pot. 3. Drape the dough over the strawberries. 4. Cover the pot with lid. Turn dial to SLOW COOK, set temperature to HI, and set time to 40 minutes. 5. Remove the lid. Using the tip of a knife, cut the dough into 2-inch squares while still in the pot. 6. Keep the lid off and continue to cook on high for an additional 40 minutes. 7. When cooking is complete, serve hot.

Homemade Rocky Road Candy

Prep Time: 10 minutes | Cook Time: 2 hours | Serves: 12

2 (24-ounce) packages semisweet chocolate chips
¼ cup solid vegetable shortening

1 (8-ounce) bag chopped walnuts
½ (10-ounce) bag mini marshmallows

1. Combine the chocolate chips, vegetable shortening, and walnuts in the pot. 2. Cover the pot with lid. Turn dial to SLOW COOK, set temperature to LO, and set time to 1 hour. 3. Stir, then cook for an additional hour, stirring every 15 minutes. 4. Stir in the marshmallows. Drop by rounded teaspoons onto wax or parchment paper. Allow 30 minutes to 1 hour to harden, then store in a sealed container, separated by layers of wax paper, at cool room temperature for up to a week, or freeze for up to 1 month.

Flavorful Double Chocolate Brownies

Prep Time: 10 minutes | Cook Time: 3½ hours | Serves: 12

Cooking spray
¾ cup unbleached flour
½ cup cocoa powder
½ teaspoon baking powder
½ teaspoon kosher salt
½ cup (1 stick) unsalted butter, cut up

1 cup sugar
2 eggs, lightly beaten
1 teaspoon vanilla extract
¾ cup semisweet chocolate chips
½ cup chopped walnuts (optional)

1. Lightly spray the pot with cooking spray. Cut a circle of parchment paper and place on the bottom of the pot. Lightly press down paper, then lightly spray parchment as well. 2. In a small mixing bowl, whisk together flour, baking powder, cocoa, and salt. Set aside. 3. In a medium-sized heat-safe bowl, melt butter in microwave at 100 percent power for 45 seconds. Stir until completely melted. Whisk in sugar, then eggs. 4. Using a rubber spatula, stir the prepared flour mixture into the butter mixture just until incorporated. Fold in chocolate chips, vanilla extract, and chopped walnuts, if using. Spread chocolate mixture on bottom of prepared pot. 5. Cover the pot with lid. Turn dial to SLOW COOK, set temperature to LO, and set time to 3 hours. The outer edges will be dry with the center still wet. Leave cover off and continue to cook for another 30 minutes. The center should still be underdone, but will firm up as it cools. 6. Let cool completely. Run a table knife around the edges of the brownies. Carefully lift the brownies from the pot and let cool completely before cutting.

Fluffy Blueberry Muffin Cake

Prep Time: 15 minutes | Cook Time: 4-6 hours | Serves: 10

Cooking spray
3 cups almond flour
½ cup 2% fat plain Greek yogurt
¼ cup powdered erythritol sweetener of your choice
3 large eggs
2 to 3 teaspoons grated lemon zest

1½ teaspoons baking powder
1 teaspoon vanilla extract
½ teaspoon baking soda
¼ teaspoon salt
1 cup fresh or frozen blueberries

1. Coat the pot generously with cooking spray. 2. In a large bowl, mix together the yogurt, erythritol, almond flour, lemon zest, baking powder, eggs, vanilla, baking soda, and salt until well blended. Carefully fold in the blueberries. 3. Pour the batter into the pot. 4. Place a paper towel between the pot and the lid to cut down on any condensation that develops. 5. Cover the pot with lid. Turn dial to SLOW COOK, set temperature to LO, and set time to 4 hours. Cook on low for 4 to 6 hours or on high for 2 to 3 hours, or until a toothpick inserted in the center comes out clean. 6. When cooking is complete, serve and enjoy.

Fresh Strawberry Cobbler

Prep Time: 15 minutes | Cook Time: 4-6 hours | Serves: 8

Cooking spray
2 cups fresh strawberries
3 tablespoons powdered erythritol sweetener of your choice, divided
1 large egg

½ cup coconut oil
1 teaspoon vanilla
1 cup coconut flour
1 cup almond flour

1. Coat the pot generously with cooking spray. 2. Place the berries on the bottom of the pot and sprinkle them with 2 tablespoons of erythritol. 3. In a large bowl, mix together the egg, coconut oil, remaining 1 tablespoon erythritol, and the vanilla. Fold in the coconut flour and the almond flour, mixing well until a thick batter forms. 4. Spread the batter evenly on top of the berries with the back of a spoon or your hand and press it down lightly. 5. Place a paper towel between the pot and the lid to cut down on any condensation that develops. 6. Cover the pot with lid. Turn dial to SLOW COOK, set temperature to LO, and set time to 4 hours. Cook on low for 4 to 6 hours or on high for 2 to 3 hours, or until a toothpick inserted in the center comes out clean. 7. When cooking is complete, serve and enjoy.

Light Crustless Pumpkin Pie

Prep Time: 10 minutes | Cook Time: 2-4 hours | Serves: 4

Cooking spray
1 (15-ounce) can pumpkin purée (without salt)
4 large eggs, beaten
½ cup whole milk

¼ cup powdered erythritol sweetener of your choice
1½ teaspoons vanilla
1 teaspoon pumpkin pie spice
½ teaspoon salt

1. Coat the pot generously with cooking spray. 2. In a large bowl, mix together the pumpkin, vanilla, eggs, milk, erythritol, pumpkin pie spice, and salt. Spread the mixture evenly in the bottom of pot. 3. Place a paper towel between the pot and the lid to cut down on any condensation that develops. 4. Cover the pot with lid. Turn dial to SLOW COOK, set temperature to LO, and set time to 2 hours. Cook on low for 2 to 4 hours or on high for 1 to 2 hours. 5. When cooking is complete, serve and enjoy.

As we conclude the Ninja Foodi PossibleCooker Pro Cookbook, we celebrate the new adventure in the kitchen. The cookbook highlighted the fundamentals and recipes and empowered you to use the Ninja Foodi PossibleCooker Pro fully.

In each dish you prepare in your kitchen, find the joy of creativity and the celebration of flavors. The Ninja Foodi PossibleCooker Pro is your friend in the kitchen, giving you a chance to experiment with different recipes. Remember, cooking is a learning process, and the more you do it, the more you learn and perfect. Go out there and fill your kitchen with the unique aromas. Let Ninja Foodi PossibleCooker Pro change your experience in the kitchen. Happy cooking!

Appendix 1 Measurement Conversion Chart

WEIGHT EQUIVALENTS

US STANDARD	METRIC (APPROXINATE)
1 ounce	28 g
2 ounces	57 g
5 ounces	142 g
10 ounces	284 g
15 ounces	425 g
16 ounces (1 pound)	455 g
1.5pounds	680 g
2pounds	907 g

TEMPERATURES EQUIVALENTS

FAHRENHEIT(F)	CELSIUS(C) (APPROXIMATE)
225 °F	107 °C
250 °F	120 °C
275 °F	135 °C
300 °F	150 °C
325 °F	160 °C
350 °F	180 °C
375 °F	190 °C
400 °F	205 °C
425 °F	220 °C
450 °F	235 °C
475 °F	245 °C
500 °F	260 °C

VOLUME EQUIVALENTS (DRY)

US STANDARD	METRIC (APPROXIMATE)
⅛ teaspoon	0.5 mL
¼ teaspoon	1 mL
½ teaspoon	2 mL
¾ teaspoon	4 mL
1 teaspoon	5 mL
1 tablespoon	15 mL
¼ cup	59 mL
½ cup	118 mL
¾ cup	177 mL
1 cup	235 mL
2 cups	475 mL
3 cups	700 mL
4 cups	1 L

VOLUME EQUIVALENTS (LIQUID)

US STANDARD	US STANDARD (OUNCES)	METRIC (APPROXIMATE)
2 tablespoons	1 fl.oz	30 mL
¼ cup	2 fl.oz	60 mL
½ cup	4 fl.oz	120 mL
1 cup	8 fl.oz	240 mL
1½ cup	12 fl.oz	355 mL
2 cups or 1 pint	16 fl.oz	475 mL
4 cups or 1 quart	32 fl.oz	1 L
1 gallon	128 fl.oz	4 L

Appendix 2 Recipes Index

A

Apple & Peach Crumble 91

Apple and Pear Compote with Cranberries 90

Apple Oatmeal 16

Asian-Style Meatballs 44

Authentic Caribbean Chicken Curry 59

B

Baked Sweet Potatoes 45

Balsamic Bacon and Vegetable Medley 33

Balsamic Braised Red Cabbage 32

Balsamic Brussels Sprouts with Cranberries 28

Banana-Pineapple Foster 92

Barbecue Pulled Chicken 51

Barbecued Pinto Beans 43

Basil Spinach Oatmeal 14

Bay Beef Bone Broth 62

Beef and Bell Peppers Stew 63

Beef Chili with Black Beans 79

Beef Stew with Vegetables 66

Beer Cheese Soup 86

Beet and Spinach Frittata 12

Best Cauliflower Fried Rice 36

Breakfast Quinoa with Walnuts and Apples 19

Breakfast Strawberry and Banana Quinoa 14

Brown Sugar Glazed Carrots 30

Buffalo Cauliflower Chili 27

Buffalo Chicken Lettuce Wraps with Cherry Tomatoes 51

Buttered Cauliflower Mash 29

Buttered Cheese Grits 21

C

Cabbage with Bacon and Pearl Onions 29

Caramelized Peach Steel-Cut Oats 17

Carrot Barley Soup 81

Cheese Meatballs in Tomato Sauce 67

Cheesy Jalapeño Poppers 46

Cheesy Raspberry Cookies 92

Cheesy Stuffed Tomatoes 27

Cheesy Turkery-Stuffed Peppers 54

Cherry and Pumpkin Seed Granola 12

Chicken Noodle Soup 86

Chicken Rice Soup 86

Chile Cheese Dip 47

Chili Chicken Fajita Soup 87

Chili Cranberry Turkey Meatballs 58

Chili Pork Tenderloin 62

Chocolate Chip Lava Cake 90

Cinnamon Carrot Pudding 92

Citrus Beets 30

Classic Beef Meatloaf 69

Classic Eggplant Caponata 43

Classic Eggplant Parmigiana 42

Classic Harvard Beets and Onions 25

Classic Huevos Rancheros 17

Classic Jambalaya 54

Classic Steak Diane 64

Coconut Almond and Cherry Granola 18

Coconut Chai Custard 95

Cod with Pesto Topping and White Bean Ratatouille 76

Comforting Maple Banana Sundaes 93

Comforting Parmesan Mushroom Risotto 38

Cream Cheese Peach Casserole 19

Creamed" Spinach 33

Creamy Garlic Parmesan Chicken 50

Creamy Zucchini Soup 82

Crunchy Keto Granola 16

Crustless Quiche Lorraine 20

Curried Pork Chops with Bell Peppers 64

Curried Squash with Garlic 30

D

Delicious Beef Enchilada Casserole 66

Delicious Chocolate Lava Cake 97

Delicious Cuban Chicken 57

Delicious Eggs in Purgatory 14

Delicious Onion Chutney 41

Delicious Udon Noodle Soup with Vegetables 25

Delicious Vegetarian Stuffed Peppers 33

E

Easy Braised Leeks 31

Easy Challah French Toast Casserole 19

Easy Teriyaki Chicken 60

F

Flavorful Chicken Marsala 57

Flavorful Double Chocolate Brownies 98

Flavorful Mediterranean Vegetable Stew 31

Flavorful Salmon Ratatouille 74

Flavorful Stuffed Sweet Potatoes 23

Fluffy Blueberry Muffin Cake 99

French Toast with Mixed Berries 18

Fresh Chipotle Ranch Chicken Pizza 42

Fresh Fig and Ginger Spread 45

Fresh Strawberry Cobbler 99

Fresh Tomato and Feta Frittata 20

G

Garlic Cauliflower Mashed "Potatoes" 28

Garlic Polenta with Fresh Vegetables 37

Garlic Shrimp and Grits 75

Garlic Turkey and Wild Rice 56

Garlicky Turkey Breasts 53

Golden Almond Cake 94

Greek Frittata with Olives and Artichoke Hearts 11

Ground Turkey and Vegetables 52

Ground Turkey Spaghetti Squash Casserole 60

H

Hearty Beef Stew 80

Hearty Red Wine Beef Stew 71

Hearty Salmon Meatloaf 74

Hearty White Bean, Chicken & Apple Cider Chili 51

Herbed Garlic Smashed Potatoes 26

Herbed Pork Loin with Dried Fruit 64

Herbed Vegetable Broth 23

Homemade Rocky Road Candy 98

Homemade Sephardic Cholent 72

Homemade Southwestern Veggie Bowl 35

Homemade Stuffed Grape Leaves 45

Honey Teriyaki Chicken 56

Honeyed Apple Bread Pudding 11

Honeyed Pineapple Chicken Wings 41

Hot Everything Stew 79

I

Indian Spiced Brown Rice with Lamb 39

Italian Chicken Thighs with Green Beans 49

Italian Stuffed Meatloaf 68

J

Jerk Chicken Thighs 53

K

Korean-Style Beef Lettuce Wraps 63

L

Lamb in Coconut Curry Sauce 72

Lemon Butter Cake 93

Lemon Garlic Asparagus 24

Lemon-Garlic Chicken 54

Lemony Chickpea Snackers 47

Lemony Garlic Chicken Thighs 50

Light Crustless Pumpkin Pie 99

Limey Chicken Avocado Soup 88

M

Manhattan Clam Chowder 77

Mashed Root Vegetables 24

Meatball Biscuits with Cheese 42

Mediterranean Beef with Pearl Barley 70

Mediterranean Chickpeas with Brown Rice 39

Mexican Black Beans and Brown Rice 39

Milky Pumpkin Soup 82

Minty Chocolate Truffles 95

Mixed Berry Crisp 91

Monkfish and Sweet Potatoes 76

Morning Millet with Fresh

Blueberries 13

Moroccan Lamb Stew with Nuts 85

Moroccan Lentil Soup 83

Mouthwatering Bourbon Baked Beans 38

Mouthwatering Lemon Poppy Seed Cake 94

Mushroom Barley Soup with Flanken 85

Mustard Pork and Beans 62

N

No-Bean Chili 87

Nutritious Beef Stew 83

Nutritious Chicken Zoodle Soup 87

Nutty Granola with Seeds and Dried Fruit 17

O

Old-Fashioned Vegetable Stew 83

One-Pot Chicken and Rice 36

Orange Almond Muffins 18

P

Palatable Turkey and Gravy 58

Parmesan Spaghetti Squash 47

Peach Brown Betty with Cranberries 91

Perfect Mole Chicken Bites 41

Perfect Wild Mushroom Risotto 36

Pork Chops with Sweet Potatoes 68

Pork Roast with Honey-Mustard Sauce 65

Pork Tenderloin with Peach Sauce 70

Potato and Leek Soup 84

Potato Soup 80

Pumpkin Pie Breakfast Bars 13

Q

Quinoa with Brussels Sprouts and Walnuts 25

R

Refried Pinto Beans 38

Rice Pudding with Raisins 97

Rich Sabra Compote 97

Roast Pork with Cabbage and Pears 65

Rosemary Chicken Barley Stew 81

S

Savory Chicken Fajita Chili 85

Savory Mandarin Orange Chicken 55

Savory Maple-Balsamic Lamb Shoulder 63

Shrimp Scampi with Vegetables 75

Simple Banana Cream Pie 96

Simple Cheese Omelet 20

Simple Cornish Hens in Plum Sauce 59

Slow Cooked Boston Baked Beans 35

Slow-Cooked Black Bean Soup 84

Slow-Cooked Cauliflower Mac and Cheese 30

Slow-Cooked Cheese Dip 46

Slow-Cooked Crack Chicken 59

Slow-Cooked Drunken Beans 23

Slow-Cooked Jerk Pork Chops 71

Slow-Cooked Minestrone Soup 84

Slow-Cooked Shredded Beef 68

Slow-Cooked Southwest Chicken 56

Slow-Cooked Summer Vegetables 24

Slow-Cooked Sweet and Sour Chicken 55

Slow-Cooked Sweet and Sour Scallops 77

Slow-cookedchicken Fajitas 50

Smooth Tomato Soup 82

Southwest Chicken Breasts 55

Southwestern Chicken Stew 82

Spaghetti Squash 29

Spaghetti Squash with Creamy Tomato Sauce 27

Spiced Rum-Raisin Rice Pudding 96

Spicy Italian Chickpeas 37

Spicy Rice-Stuffed Peppers 26

Spicy Rotisserie-Style Whole Chicken 52

Spinach and Feta Quiche 15

Spinach Artichoke Dip 44

Sunday Pot Roast with Gravy 69

Sweet & Sour Smoked Sausage 43

Sweet 'n' Spicy Snack Mix 46

Sweet and Sour Turkey Meatballs 44

Sweet and Spicy Chickpeas with Potatoes 37

Sweet Breakfast Cobbler 15

Sweet Mustard Chicken Fillets 52

Sweet Strawberry Pandowdy 98

T

Tasty Braised Beef and Pork with Green Salsa 66

Tasty Hash Brown Casserole 12

Tasty Peanut Butter Chocolate Cake 96

Tasty Southern Collards 32

Tasty Vanilla-Maple Farina 13

Tender Flanken Ribs in Spicy Tomato Sauce 71

Tender Pork with Potatoes and Sweet Potatoes 65

Tender Shredded Beef Ragu 69

Texas Barbecued Chicken Thighs 49

Tex-Mex Kale with Garlic Tomatoes 29

Tex-Mex Scrambled Egg 21

Thai Braised Chicken Thighs 58

Thai Green Curry with Tofu 26

Thai Panang Duck Curry 57

Three-Grain Granola with Nuts 15

Thyme Salmon with Zucchini and Carrot 76

Traditional Beef Cholent 70

Traditional Chicken Cordon Bleu 60

Tuna and Potato Casserole 74

Turkey and Broccoli Slaw Soup 88

Turkey Meatballs in Tomato Sauce 53

Tuscan-Style Chicken and White Bean Stew 81

V

Vanilla Coconut Yogurt 90

Vanilla Lemon Custard 93

Vanilla Zucchini-Carrot Bread 16

Vegan Black Bean Stew 79

Vegan White Bean Cassoulet 31

W

Wheat Berry Chicken Casserole 49

White Fish in Curried Tomato Sauce 75

Whole Grain Rigatoni with Broccoli and Peas 35

Wild Rice and Vegetable Soup 80

Y

Yellow Squash Casserole with Crackers 28

Yucatec-Style Roasted Pork 67

Yummy Pumpkin Spice Pudding 95

Z

Zucchini and Cherry Tomato Frittata 11

Zucchini Ragout with Spinach 32

Made in United States
Troutdale, OR
10/31/2024

24339941R00067